Why Do You Need this New Edition?

If you're wondering why you should buy this third edition of *The Elements of Technical Writing*, here are seven good reasons!

1. New coverage of technological concerns include discussions of ethics, electronic delivery, and the formatting of online documents in order to provide you with **up-to-date perspectives on today's communication environments** (Chapters 1, 4, 5, and 10).

2. New coverage of global communication offers you **a broader understanding of increasingly diverse work environments** (Chapters 1 and 6).

3. New end-of-chapter assignments include an individual project and a collaborative project that build cumulatively throughout Part One, allowing you to **work through a single large assignment as you move through the book.**

4. New end-of-chapter short activities that can be assigned in class or as homework enable you to **practice concepts and extend thinking** both individually and collaboratively.

5. Increased coverage of collaborative writing will help you **understand different kinds of workplace collaboration,** including working with subject matter experts and writing as a member of a team (Chapters 1 and 4).

6. New coverage of documenting research frames the discussion of **crediting sources as a consideration of ethics,** helping you understand why—not just how—professionals cite (Chapter 7).

7. Increased coverage of rhetorical concepts throughout Part One helps you **produce more effective documents** by considering your audience, purpose, and communication situation as you plan and draft.

The Elements of Technical Writing

The Elements of Technical Writing

Third Edition

Thomas E. Pearsall
Emeritus, University of Minnesota

Kelli Cargile Cook
Utah State University

Longman
New York San Francisco Boston
London Toronto Sydney Tokyo Singapore Madrid
Mexico City Munich Paris Cape Town Hong Kong Montreal

Acquisitions Editor: Lauren A. Finn
Marketing Coordinator: Bonnie Gill
Production Manager: Savoula Amanatidis
Project Coordination, Text Design, and Electronic Page Makeup:
    Nesbitt Graphics, Inc.
Cover Design Manager: Wendy Ann Fredericks
Senior Manufacturing Buyer: Roy L. Pickering, Jr.
Printer and Binder: Courier Corporation—Westford
Cover Printer: Lehigh-Phoenix Color Corporation

Library of Congress Cataloging-in-Publication Data

Pearsall, Thomas E.
  The elements of technical writing / Thomas E. Pearsall,
[consultant] Kelli Cargile Cook. -- 3rd ed.
    p. cm.
  Previous ed.: 2nd ed., Boston : Allyn and Bacon. Thomas E. Pearsall, 2000.
  Includes bibliographical references and index.
  ISBN-13: 978-0-205-58381-2
  ISBN-10: 0-205-58381-4
  1. Technical writing. I. Title.
  T11.P392 2009
  808'.0666--dc22
                              2009020335

1 2 3 4 5 6 7 8 9 10—CW—12 11 10 09

Longman
is an imprint of

ISBN-13: 978-0-205-58381-2
ISBN-10:   0-205-58381-4

www.pearsonhighered.com

Contents

PART TWO

The Formats of Technical Writing   101

8   Elements of Reports   102

9   Formats of Reports   123

Preface

Technical writing, purely and simply, is writing about subjects in technical disciplines. Whether agriculture, economics, engineering, or zoology, a technical discipline will have its *technics*—that is, its theories, principles, arts, and skills. It will generate reports and correspondence. The hallmark of such reports and correspondence is that they present objective data to *convince,* rather than using emotion to *persuade.*

People in every technical discipline will propose research and then report progress and results. In addition, people will instruct, transmit information, and argue for the validity of their opinions. Such is the stuff of technical writing, and such is the stuff of this book.

Changes in the Third Edition

The changes made in this edition reflect the ever-changing nature of technical writing and address comments received from reviewers of the previous edition.

- New coverage of technological concerns include discussions of ethics, electronic delivery, and the formatting of online documents in order to provide students with up-to-date perspectives on today's communication environments (Chapters 1, 4, 5, and 10).

- New coverage of global communication offers students a broader understanding of increasingly diverse work environments (Chapters 1 and 6).

- New coverage of documenting research frames the discussion of crediting sources as a consideration of ethics, helping students understand why—not just how—professionals cite (Chapter 7).

- New end-of-chapter short activities that can be assigned in class or as homework enable students to expand their understanding of key chapter concepts.

- New end-of-chapter assignments include both individual and team assignments to help students apply key chapter concepts in writing. An individual project and a collaborative project build cumulatively throughout Part One, teaching students a process for applying the elements of technical writing described in these chapters and allowing them to work through a single large assignment as they move through the book. The assignments in Chapters 8 through 10 encourage students to repeat the process in more extensive writing projects.

- Increased coverage of rhetorical concepts throughout Part One helps students produce more effective documents by considering audience, purpose, and communication situation as they plan and draft.

- Increased coverage of collaborative writing helps students understand different kinds of workplace collaboration, including working with subject matter experts and writing as a member of a team (Chapters 1 and 4).

The appendixes, which contained writing models, have been eliminated. This edition suggests that students find their own examples to illustrate how writing tasks vary and change in response to different workplace audiences and situations. Instructors who would like their students to review examples and models are encouraged to request access to *MyTechCommLab*, an electronic resource that contains links to an archive of more than 80 technical writing samples. Please go to www.mytechcommlab.com and follow the instructions for first-time users.

Plan of the Book

This third edition contains seven chapters on the principles of technical writing and three on the formats—ten chapters in all. The first seven chapters provide a recommended process for writing technical documents while the last three chapters offer conventional guidelines to consider when writing technical reports and correspondence.

The seven chapters in Part One present the essential principles of good technical writing:

- Chapter 1, Know Your Purpose and Your Writing Situation
- Chapter 2, Know Your Audience and Their Situation
- Chapter 3, Choose and Organize Your Content Around Your Purpose and Audience
- Chapter 4, Write Clearly and Precisely
- Chapter 5, Use Good Page Design
- Chapter 6, Think Visually
- Chapter 7, Write Ethically

These principles can support your work each time you write, and you will find yourself cycling through this process for most workplace writing assignments.

Part Two covers some of the structural and organizational features of technical writing:

- Chapter 8, Elements of Reports, describes elements such as title pages, abstracts, introductions, and documentation.

- Chapter 9, Formats of Reports, provides formats for major reports, such as research reports, recommendation reports, and proposals.

- Chapter 10, Formats of Correspondence, shows how to format letters and memorandums and how to write letters of application and résumés.

Acknowledgments

In many places, the sources of ideas and materials are acknowledged. Most often, ideas have come from a combination of places that would be impossible to document. They are the materials that those of us in technical writing have freely shared with each other for years. But some of the individuals who must be thanked include Paul Anderson, Virginia Book, W. Earl Britton, David Carson, Mary Coney, Donald Cunningham, Sam Dragga, Herman Estrin, Jay Gould, John Harris, Ken Houp, Ann Laster, Fred MacIntosh, Victoria Mikelonis, John Mitchell, Nell Ann Pickett, Janice Redish, Tom Sawyer, Jim Souther, Elizabeth Tebeaux, John Walter,

Tom Warren, Arthur Walzer, and Mike White. Blessings on them all, and double blessings on anyone neglected to mention.

Thanks to those professors who reviewed the previous edition of this book and made many useful suggestions for this new edition: May Charles, Belmont Technical College; Katherine Hall, Roger Williams University; Mary Jae Kleckner, Mid-State Technical College, Wisconsin Rapids; Stuart Selber, Pennsylvania State University–University Park; and Clay Spinuzzi, University of Texas at Austin. Thanks also to colleagues who reviewed earlier editions: Dan Jones, University of Central Florida; Carolyn Plumb, Montana State University; Norma Procopiow, Columbia Union College; Ricky W. Telg, University of Florida; and Art Walzer, University of Minnesota.

Thomas E. Pearsall
Kelli Cargile Cook

The Elements of Technical Writing

PART ONE

The Seven Principles of Technical Writing

1. Know Your Purpose and Your Writing Situation

2. Know Your Audience and Their Situation

3. Choose and Organize Your Content Around Your Purpose and Audience

4. Write Clearly and Precisely

5. Use Good Page Design

6. Think Visually

7. Write Ethically

1

Know Your Purpose and Your Writing Situation

Workplace writing is not accomplished in a vacuum. It always has a context in which it is written and read. Recognizing that context is your first job as a technical writer. Every time you begin a writing task, you should know your writing purpose, your writing situation, your audience, and their situation. These four aspects determine your writing context. In this chapter, you'll take the first step in identifying your writing context: identifying your purpose for writing and considering your own writing situation.

Your Purpose

To begin identifying and understanding your purpose, answer these questions: What do you want your reader to do or accomplish after reading your writing? More specifically, what goal do you have in writing? What objective do you wish to achieve? What result do you hope for? What do you want to accomplish? In short, all these questions address what you see as your *purpose* in whatever it is you are writing, whether an e-mail message, a résumé, or a major report. Basically, technical writing has only two purposes: (1) to inform and (2) to argue. Given that, consider these two examples of purpose:

> To inform mechanical engineers about the sturdy foam metals becoming available in the marketplace

> To inform mechanical engineers about the sturdy foam metals becoming available in the marketplace and to argue for the superiority of foam metal over solid metal in certain applications

The first purpose—to inform—will be met by writing a report that objectively describes the foam metals becoming available. The report that satisfies the second purpose—to argue—should be no less objective but will contain an argument that evaluates the solids and the foams to demonstrate the superiority claimed. For example, the argument might compare and contrast the solids and the foams in certain applications. (See Chapter 9 for various formats used in informing and arguing.)

Many variations on reports that inform and argue exist in technical writing. For instance, definitions and descriptions are largely informative. So are written instructions, for the most part, although argument may play a role, as in this example:

> This new way of dry cleaning is more environmentally friendly than the old way.

But much of technical writing is argumentative. Research reports inform their readers of the facts that have been uncovered and then argue for the reliability of the conclusions drawn from those facts. Similarly, recommendation reports inform, analyze, evaluate, and draw conclusions that support their recommendations. Proposals argue for engaging an organization to do a certain task. And so on.

To succeed as a writer, you must clearly envision your purpose for whatever it is you are writing. You are more likely to succeed in achieving your purpose if you state it in writing:

> I want to convince the executives of Elmont Bank to accept my company's proposal to update the software used by their tellers in reporting bank transactions.

> I want to demonstrate to the upper management of Dickens' Sporting Goods Company the feasibility of using titanium foam in the manufacture of golf club heads.

> Our team's writing purpose is to instruct the tellers of Elmont Bank in how to use the new software we have installed for their use in reporting bank transactions.

Our group's purpose for writing is to explain to the technicians who manufacture golf clubs for Dickens' Sporting Goods Company the techniques required for working with titanium foam.

Your Situation

You probably noticed as you read these purpose statements that some of them are written from the perspective of a single writer while others relate to writing tasks that several individuals complete. Frequently in workplace writing, individuals must work with others to research, write, and deliver their documents. In other words, it takes a team to accomplish a writing purpose, and usually the team works with specific constraints or restrictions that require members to collaborate creatively with each other and with technology in order to succeed. Before you begin a writing task, you should consider your own workplace writing situation. Here are a few key questions that can help you describe your writing situation and plan for the advantages and disadvantages it may bring with it:

- **Production questions:** How much time do you have to complete your writing assignment? What kinds of tasks do you need to complete? What resources (books, software, people) do you need to complete your assignment? What is your budget for getting these resources? If your budget is restricted, how will you accomplish your tasks within these limits?

- **Collaboration questions:** Will you be writing alone or collaborating with others as you write? Will your collaborators be located in a nearby office or in an office located on the other side of the globe? When you work with others, how will you divide tasks among team members, and how will you deal with differences of opinion?

- **Technology questions:** If you are collaborating, how will you use technology to support your work? Will you exchange electronic files with others, save files on a common network drive, send them through e-mail, post them on a wiki (web-based software that allows users to collaborate by adding, deleting, and editing content), or share text in some other way?

- **Cultural questions:** What cultural differences do you and your collaborators have? How will you identify and work with these differences?

These are just a few of the questions you should answer before you begin to write. If you work out these details during the planning stage, then writing the document will be much smoother and easier. A preliminary document that can help you organize all the information you gather about your purpose and writing situation is called a **work plan.** After considering your writing purpose and situation, you could complete the following information on a work plan: purpose of your writing task, personnel (person or persons who do the writing), resources needed, tasks to be accomplished, schedule, and budget.

The example below illustrates how your work plan might look:

Work Plan

Project Title: New Instructions for Banking Solutions Manual

Purpose for Writing: To instruct the tellers of Elmont Bank in how to use the new software we have installed for reporting bank transactions

Personnel: Jamie Grant, technical writer, and Marcus Xavier, software engineer. Jamie will be telecommuting three days a week, so we will need to meet on Tuesdays or Fridays each week. Jamie's e-mail is jgrant@bsolutions.com, and Marcus's e-mail is mxavier@bsolutions.com. Both can be reached through the company phone line. Jamie's extension is 437 and Marcus's is 971.

Resources:

1. Copy of new software, Banking Solutions
2. Electronic copy of old software instruction manual that we will be updating
3. Space on company network drive to share files as we update manual

Tasks to Be Completed:

1. Review old manual and identify information that no longer applies to new version of Banking Solutions—Marcus and Jamie

(continued)

(continued)

2. Insert new instructions in Chapters 1, 2, and 5 for updated functions—Jamie

3. Write introduction that explains changes in the program and manual—Jamie

4. Review changes for accuracy—Marcus

5. Test changes with group of tellers—Jamie

6. Revise after testing—Jamie and Marcus

7. Complete final review—Jamie and Marcus

8. Submit final draft to production team for final edit and publication—Jamie

Schedule:

Revision review—August 15–31

Drafting—September 1–14

Testing—September 15–20

Post-test revisions—September 21–30

Instructions to production team for editing and publication—October 1

Software release date—October 15

Budget:

This project should be completed during regular work hours, so it will not be billed separately.

Jamie is assigned to work on this project for 20 hours per week, and Marcus is assigned to work on it for 5 hours per week.

Writing a work plan can assist you in understanding your writing purpose and situation, but this step is just the beginning of the process. You must also consider your audience and their situation. We explore these concepts in the next chapter, Know Your Audience and Their Situation.

ACTIVITIES

1. Bring an example of technical writing to class (for example, a letter, a brochure, a flyer, a manual) and analyze it for audience, purpose, and writing situation. What can you tell about the writer's purpose and situation from analyzing the document?

2. Work with a classmate to prepare a five-minute oral report for your class in which you present and describe a technical writing document. Before you begin, quickly sketch your presentation using the work plan model in this chapter. When you have planned your presentation, deliver it.

CHAPTER ASSIGNMENTS

At the end of Chapters 1–7, you will find two assignments: an individual assignment and a group assignment. These assignments are designed to give you practice in using the element of technical writing described in each chapter. The assignments are cumulative, beginning with Chapter 1 and concluding in Chapter 7. You should complete the individual assignments on your first pass through the chapters. After you complete these assignments, your instructor may ask you to cycle through the chapters again, completing the group assignments.

After completing both assignment cycles, your instructor may assign other writing tasks, such as those described at the end of Chapters 8, 9, and 10. Even though these assignments will not cycle you directly through the steps described in Chapters 1–7, continue to apply these guidelines and you will soon find you are developing good practices for completing any technical writing assignment.

Assignment 1 for Individual Writers: The Analytical Report

Your writing situation: You have recently been employed as a technical writer at a small start-up company. To reduce overhead and commuting costs, employees in your company have asked management to allow them to work remotely from home one to three days a week. Management is interested in this proposal, but they are concerned that employees will be unable to complete team assignments if they are not working together in the same office space during the same hours. You have heard about software called groupware that allows teams to work together over the Internet, and you mention this idea to your supervisor. She asks you to investigate this possibility and write a short report (in the form of a memo, no longer than two or three pages), explaining what groupware is and analyzing how it might be used to support remote workers.

Specifically, your supervisor wants your report to answer the following questions:

1. What is groupware or Web-based collaborative software?

2. What are the most popular groupware products?

3. What are the features of the most popular groupware products?

4. What do these features allow users to do, or what kinds of tasks can groups complete using these products?

Your assignment for this chapter: Before you begin your work, familiarize yourself with the elements of informal reports by reading Chapter 8; with the format of an analytical report by reading Chapter 9, pp. 130–136; and with memo format by reading Chapter 10, pp. 153–154. When you have completed your reading, begin to draft your work plan for this assignment, indicating your assignment's title, purpose, personnel, resources needed, and tasks.

Assignment 2 for a Writing Team: The Recommendation Report

Your writing situation: After reviewing your work on groupware, your supervisor presented your report to management. Now everyone wants more information about groupware possibilities. Your next assignment is to work with a team to research and recommend a specific groupware application for remote workers at your company.

The best choice for your company will be an inexpensive or free application that allows workers to write collaboratively, share files, access calendars and other project management tools, and communicate with instant messaging or e-mail. The groupware application should also be very easy to use and require very little training.

Your assignment for this chapter: To complete the recommendation report, choose three to five of the best groupware products you and your team can find, compare and contrast them using the criteria for selection, and recommend the product you think will work best for your company. Support your recommendation with data from your research, and present your findings in a formal recommendation report.

Review the elements of formal reports in Chapter 8 and the format of analytical recommendation reports in Chapter 9. Meet with your teammates to draft your work plan for this assignment, indicating your assignment's title, purpose, personnel, resources needed, and tasks. You will be able to complete the schedule and budget of the work plan after reading and discussing the next chapter.

2

Know Your Audience and Their Situation

Good writers are aware of their audiences, and they consider their audiences' situations whenever they write. Understanding audiences not only means knowing who they are but also knowing where they are and what they will be doing when they read your writing. Audiences read and respond to writing in all kinds of workplace settings, such as reading on computer screens, reviewing printed safety procedures on a warehouse floor, checking e-mail on a commuter train, or even listening to an instructional podcast while exercising or eating lunch. Thinking about your writing as a product that is delivered to a specific audience working in a specific context will help you to make choices that improve your audience's ability to understand and respond to your writing as you intend.

As you visualize your readers, consider these things:

- Their concerns and characteristics
- Their education, experiences, and workplace locations
- Their attitudes toward your purpose and information

Concerns and Characteristics

Figure 2.1 summarizes the concerns and characteristics of five major audiences you may face as a technical writer and indicates some ways to satisfy the needs of each. For example, notice that executives read primarily for the purpose of making decisions. Thus, an executive will be

Audience	Concerns and Characteristics
Laypersons	• Read for learning and interest • Have more interest in practice than theory • Need help with science and mathematics • Enjoy and learn from human interest • Require background and definitions • Need simplicity • Learn from simple graphics
Executives	• Read to make decisions • Have more interest in practice than theory • Need plain language • Learn from simple graphics • Need information on people, profits, and environment • Expect implications, conclusions, and recommendations to be expressed clearly • Read selectively—skimming and scanning • Have self-interests as well as corporate interests
Technicians	• Read for how-to information • Expect emphasis on practical matters • May have limitations in mathematics and theory • May expect theory if higher level
Experts	• Read for how and why things work • Need and want theory • Will read selectively • Can handle mathematics and terminology of field • Expect graphics to display results • Need new terms defined • Expect inferences and conclusions to be clearly but cautiously expressed and well-supported
Combined	• One person may combine the attributes of several audiences • Readers may consist of representatives of several audiences

FIGURE 2.1   Audience Concerns and Characteristics

disappointed by a report that does not clearly state the author's conclusions and back up those conclusions with sufficient but succinct information. Notice also that executives read selectively, skimming and scanning materials. Picture an officer in a large company, facing a desk piled high with reports. Looking over these reports, the officer can make various judgments and exercise options accordingly:

> This entire report directly concerns decisions I have to make; I need to read it carefully and evaluate the information and conclusions presented.

> Some of this report concerns my department; I better look through it and read the pertinent parts carefully.

> This report looks interesting; I better scan it.

> This report contains nothing of concern to me; I will initial and pass it on.

Using the information in this book about good page design (see Chapter 5) and formats of technical writing (see Part Two), you can support executives' thinking processes and allow them to read selectively.

Unlike executives, technicians read primarily for how-to information. For example, you operate as a technician when you consult the instruction manual for, say, your personal computer. You go to that manual to learn how to operate the computer or perhaps to solve a particular problem you are having with it. And you expect the information in the manual to be written in language you clearly understand and organized in a format you can easily access.

In similar fashion, experts read professional books, journals, and papers to keep up to date on the latest research and developments in their fields and to guide their work, and laypeople read materials that may interest or entertain them or influence their attitudes and decisions. Keeping your readers' concerns and characteristics in mind is essential to satisfying their needs and to accomplishing your own purpose.

Education, Experience, and Location

Based on our individual levels of education and experience, we all learn *vocabulary, concepts,* and *techniques* for doing things. For example, civil engineers understand that the term *safety factor* means "the margin by which a machine exceeds its required performance." The safety factor for most passenger elevators is 7.6; that is, they will carry 7.6 times the average weight of the number of passengers they are specified to carry. In addition, engineers understand the concept of *safety factor*. They could build elevators with a safety factor of 30, but the cost would be so excessive that no one could afford it. Therefore, safety factors are based on a balance of safety and cost.

When civil engineers write, they have to know which technical engineering terms and concepts their readers will likely know and not know. When writing for fellow engineers, they can assume a shared vocabulary and understanding and leave technical terms and concepts undefined and unexplained. When writing for nonengineers, however, they will have to define and explain as necessary, based on the audience's level of education and experience.

Similarly, through education and experience, we learn techniques for doing things. Consider that the technical writers who produced the computer manual you use had to estimate your knowledge of how to use a keyboard and mouse. If they estimated correctly, you will be a happy reader; if their judgment was incorrect, you will be an unhappy reader.

When you write about what you have learned through your own education and experience, you must consider how well your readers will understand the words, concepts, and techniques you write about. Accordingly, when you think your readers might need help with any of these aspects, offer it.

Finally, you should think about where your readers will be located when they read. For example, the executive will likely be sitting at a desk in a quiet office when reading a report, but a mechanic searching for help in repairing an automobile will likely be in a garage surrounded by tools, used and new parts, and noise from surrounding work. Unlike the mechanic who uses a printed manual, a student who needs help with a graphics program may turn to online help. Whatever your readers' location, your document should meet their needs in content as well as in design and media choices. Your printed document may need to be laminated if it is used in fieldwork, or it might need to be spiral bound to open easily on a worktable, depending on its preferred use. Knowing your audience and their preferences will help you to make the best choices possible for communicating your message to them.

Attitudes Toward Purpose and Information

Consider this possible situation:

> You are writing a report for your supervisor that recommends the purchase of a new, more powerful computer for the office in which the two of you work. You know that your supervisor wants to buy the computer and is looking for support to justify the purchase.

Or maybe the reverse is true:

> Your supervisor does not think the new computer is needed. In fact, she considers it a waste of money.

In the first situation, your supervisor will read your report in a positive frame of mind. If she has the sole decision-making authority to buy the computer, she may not even read the entire report carefully. Your supervisor's approach to your report will be different, however, if she needs to convince someone higher up the chain of command to buy the computer. She will still be pleased with your report but will perhaps read it with more care to make sure your argument convincingly expresses your purpose: to justify the purchase of the new computer.

In the second situation, your supervisor will be at least skeptical of both your purpose and your information; she may even be hostile. Thus, she will read carefully, looking for flaws and weaknesses in your argument for buying the computer. It will take a strong, well-supported argument to convince her.

Consider the position of someone writing technical instructions. He must acknowledge that few people approach technical instructions eagerly. Instead, they most likely want to use the instructions to find the information they need and to do so as quickly and easily as possible. Readers with this attitude want to read instructions selectively; that is, they want to read only those parts they need and skip the rest.

Suppose, for example, you are writing online instructions about how to use a software program that calculates and reports federal income tax. What kinds of information will your readers want? All of them will want to know two basic things: (1) how to install the software on their computers and (2) how to complete a standard 1040 tax form.

Beyond those two skills, however, individual readers will have different needs. For instance, some may need to know how to deal with child support payments, home office expenses, or individual retirement accounts (IRAs).

Others may need to know how to transfer information from other programs into the tax program or vice versa.

Whatever the specific interest, no one wants to read through unneeded information to get to needed information. Being forced to do so will put readers in a hostile mood. Therefore, in writing instructions, or any technical documents, ensure that the material is organized and designed to be read selectively.

As these examples indicate, people can approach reading technical documents with widely varying attitudes: agreement or hostility, trust or skepticism, passion or indifference, eagerness or reluctance. One attitude, however, is nearly universal: No one wants to linger. In our busy world, readers want to find what they need in a piece of technical writing, comprehend it, and move on. When writing a technical document, your job is to help them do just that.

When you have considered your audience and their workplace situations, you should add what you have learned to your work plan. For example, you can add categories for audience identification, education level, and workplace location. This information will help you to choose the most appropriate language for your audience, determine how much persuasion and support to include in your document, and design your document so it can be used effectively in the location where your audience works. You will learn more about these decisions as you work through later chapters, but for now, update your work plan with the information you have been able to gather so far.

The following work plan illustrates how to incorporate everything you have learned so far into a single document:

Work Plan

Project Title: HMO Folic Acid Brochure

Technical Writer: Dominic DeSoto

Purpose for Writing: My purpose is to write a brochure for the members of a health maintenance organization (HMO) that explains

(continued)

(*continued*)

the role of folic acid in preventing neural tube malformations (anencephaly and spina bifida) and describes how women of childbearing age can ensure they get sufficient folic acid in their diets to prevent such malformations during pregnancy.

Audience

Readers' concerns and characteristics: The audience I wish to reach, either directly or through relatives or friends, is women of childbearing age. Essentially, this will be an audience of laypeople who read for learning and interest. My readers probably have some concerns about good health and healthy babies, but because they don't know the dangers of neural tube malformations, they have no concerns about them. This audience will require background information and definitions along with graphics and an easy-to-read text.

Readers' education and experience in the subject area: Because a wide cross-section of U.S. society belongs to HMOs, my readers likely have an average level of education (certainly no higher than high school and perhaps as low as the eighth grade). This means I should assume that my readers have no clear knowledge of the role of folic acid in the diet or what neural tube birth malformations are.

Readers' attitudes toward my purpose: Because many people do not worry about health problems until they actually appear, I should assume a certain amount of reader indifference toward my purpose.

Personnel: I will work alone on this project and produce the brochure in approximately ten days. Mary Elizabeth Bartholomew, RN, will review the materials to make sure the information I'm including is accurate. Mary Elizabeth will need four days to review, edit, and return the brochure to me. I will also need to interview Dr. Martina Gordon before writing.

Resources and Tasks to Be Completed

1. HMO research

   a. I will go to the HMO to gather and review brochures already being used there. This review will give me a better understanding of format and design for my brochure. The new brochure will need to fit in the same storage cabinet and display as the current ones, so it needs to be the same size and shape.

   b. I will go to the HMO medical library and gather medical bulletins (both in print and online) that explain the importance of folic acid during pregnancy and read them. If necessary, I will need to get permission to quote from these medical materials.

2. I will interview Mary Elizabeth and Dr. Martina Gordon after I have gathered print and online information to make sure I have all the information I need for the brochure.

3. When I have confirmation from Mary Elizabeth and Dr. Gordon, I will draft the brochure's content in Microsoft Word. (The HMO staff uses Word for all word processing, so my brochure needs to be created in Word so it can be updated later by the HMO staff, if necessary.)

4. I will e-mail Mary Elizabeth and attach the content. She will review the content (copy) while I begin to lay out the text.

5. While Mary Elizabeth is reviewing the copy, I will gather graphics (because the brochure will be printed in-house on a copier, I will use black and white illustrations, not color photographs or drawings).

6. When Mary Elizabeth returns the copy, I will insert it in my brochure with the graphics and return the second draft to her for review.

7. When she has reviewed the second draft, I will make any changes she recommends and then deliver it to the HMO staff for copying.

(*continued*)

(*continued*)

Schedule

Date	Task	Time Required	Assignment
2/4–2/5	Research and information gathering, including meeting with Mary Elizabeth and Dr. Gordon.	4 hours	Dominic
2/6–2/7	Write copy.	2 hours	Dominic
2/7–2/8	Review.	2 days	Mary Elizabeth
2/7–2/8	1. Create graphics, as needed, or get permissions, if necessary. 2. Design brochure, including graphics and copy.	3–4 hours	Dominic
2/11	1. Revise copy with Mary Elizabeth's recommendations (second draft). 2. Insert revised copy into brochure design.	2 hours	Dominic
2/12–2/13	Final review of completed brochure.	2 days	Mary Elizabeth
2/14	1. Make final editing changes, if necessary. 2. Deliver brochure for copying.	1 hour	Dominic

Budget

This project will take approximately fifteen hours over nine days to complete. At $25 per hour, the brochure should cost $375 to produce. The HMO will cover the cost of Mary Elizabeth's review and production of the brochure, so no additional expenses will be incurred.

ACTIVITIES

1. Imagine that you have been asked to create a health-related flyer to attract students like your classmates. The flyer's purpose is to announce a blood drive at your college and persuade students to give blood. Using the guidelines described in this chapter, interview several of your classmates and write a detailed audience analysis that helps you to shape your brochure to reach this audience most effectively. Consider questions like these: Who is the primary audience? What do you want them to do? How would you describe their education level, attitudes, and beliefs? Where would your audience most likely see the flyer? What would attract them to read and respond to it? Share your findings with your class, and compare what you found to others' analyses. Did you all reach the same conclusions about your audience?

2. The previous activity asked you to consider your classmates as an audience. What other audiences might also see the blood drive flyer? What do you know about these audiences? How might an awareness of these audiences also shape the content and design of the flyer?

CHAPTER ASSIGNMENTS

Assignment 1 for Individual Writers: The Analytical Report

At the end of Chapter 1, you began your work plan for the analytical report you are writing. Apply what you have learned in this chapter to expand and complete your plan. Address specific characteristics of your readers that you will need to consider, and develop a schedule and budget. Use the example in this chapter as a model for your own work plan.

Assignment 2 for a Writing Team: The Recommendation Report

At the end of Chapter 1, you and your teammates drafted your preliminary work plan for the formal recommendation report you are writing. Apply what you have learned in this chapter to expand and complete your plan. Address specific characteristics of your readers that you will need to consider, and develop a schedule and budget. Be sure your schedule designates both research and writing tasks that individual group members must complete. Use the example in this chapter as a model for your own work plan.

3

Choose and Organize Your Content Around Your Purpose and Audience

If you follow the advice given in Chapters 1 and 2 about purpose and audience, you will find it easier to choose your content and organize your report. Make sure you clearly understand the following:

- Your purpose
- Your audience's concerns and characteristics
- Your audience's education and experience in the subject area
- Your audience's location and workplace situation
- Your audience's attitudes toward your purpose

Because good writing is precise, for a lengthy, important piece of writing, it is a good idea to compile this information in a work plan like the one you started in Chapter 1 and completed in Chapter 2. When you have written your work plan, you are ready to begin your research, choose your content and graphics, and organize your information in the way that best suits your purpose and audience. This chapter will provide you with recommendations for completing these tasks.

Researching Content

As the work plan at the end of Chapter 2 shows, most technical writing projects begin with research. The HMO brochure writer lists several research tasks in his work plan—talking to subject matter experts (SME) like the nurse and the medical doctor, researching medical articles, and doing Internet research for graphics. These are just a few examples of the kinds of research you can use to gather information for your technical documents. This section will introduce you to the most common research strategies technical writers use.

In the workplace, technical writers frequently work with others to gather information for their documents. For example, a technical writer might interview a computer software developer to learn how to use a new piece of software, or she might talk to an engineer to gather information for a project proposal. These SMEs may provide the writer with notes and preliminary documents to begin their drafts, but most of the time, information is gathered through face-to-face conversations, phone calls, instant messaging, or e-mails. Communicating with others to gather information is called primary research because the technical writer is gathering information firsthand.

Writers sometimes conduct their own experiments to learn about the object or technology they have been assigned to write about. In these cases, they take a product sample and play with it, trying to use it as their readers would. Considering their readers' education, experiences, and situations, they write about what the product can do. Writers may also test their own descriptions and instructions to make sure they work for their readers. This is called usability testing, and it is commonly done to make sure the writing is accurate, clear, and easy to use.

When writers use research that another person has conducted, they are using secondary research. Technical writers use secondary research when they learn about their subjects by reading reports, reviewing previous versions of software documentation, or doing Internet research. With secondary research, they learn from what others have written. Secondary research is an important method for gathering information, but careful technical writers always check for valid, authoritative resources. This is especially important when using the

Internet to gather resources. To evaluate an Internet resource, ask the following questions:

1. What does the URL tell you? Is the URL associated with an educational site (.edu), an organizational site (.org), or a commercial site (.com)? Recognizing what domain the site belongs to can help you evaluate the author's purpose in posting the information.
2. Is the author identified, and is the author's authority established and credible?
3. Is the resource dated? If it is dated, is the information current?
4. Does the information on the page appear to be balanced?
5. Is the information on the page referenced to other pages or links? If so, check these resources as well.

If the Internet resource is current, authoritative, and credible, then you can likely trust its content. For more guidelines on evaluating Internet resources, use an Internet search engine with the keywords "evaluating Web sources" and you will find more easy-to-use guidelines.

Another form of secondary research is referring to past examples of similar organizational documents (sometimes called *legacy documents*), to see what conventions and strategies other writers have used to reach similar audiences. Using legacy documents can save writers time because they may have content, like organizational profiles, that can be recycled for the new document. Writers may also use research to find graphics. Anytime writers borrow ideas, texts, or graphics from others—whether the borrowed information is from a primary or secondary source—they credit the original work and, if necessary, seek permission to use the work. You will learn more about the importance of permissions in Chapter 7.

Whether you use primary or secondary research to gather information for your technical writing document, you will probably gather much more than you are actually able to use. For this reason, your next step is extremely important: choosing the best content.

Choosing Content

The principle you should follow in choosing content is simple: *Choose the level and amount of content that is needed to fulfill your purpose and your readers' needs—but no more than that.*

Even though this principle seems simple, it is not easy to follow. Most writers—particularly those who are experts in the subjects they are writing about—tell readers more than they really want to know. For example, most owners of DVRs do not care to know anything about DVRs except how to set them and use them. Giving readers additional information is not only a waste of time, but it may actually get in the way of conveying the information they really do need.

Likewise, experts in a scientific field reading a report of an experiment probably want information that would not concern or interest nonexperts. On the other hand, to be credible and convincing in an argument, you have to provide sufficient information to demonstrate that your conclusions are probably correct.

In other words, choosing content requires thought and judgment on your part. It requires putting yourself in your readers' place. Perhaps the best way to do that is to ask the questions that readers might have. Looking at the HMO example again will illustrate the process.

Imagine for a moment that you are one of the readers of the HMO brochure about folic acid and neural tube malformations. You may be a woman of childbearing age, or perhaps you have friends or relatives who fall into that group. What do you want to know? Your list might include these questions:

What are neural tube malformations?

Will folic acid prevent neural tube malformations?

How much folic acid is required?

When do I need to take folic acid?

Why are neural tube malformations dangerous?

Who is in danger?

What foods or food supplements will provide a sufficient supply of folic acid?

You should choose content that will answer such questions for your readers. Choose enough content so that your answers will be credible and convincing, but do not overload your readers with too much technical detail. For instance, to answer the last question on the list, tell your readers that foods containing folic acid include dark green leafy vegetables, fruits, beans, whole grains, and breakfast cereals. Indicate, perhaps in a table, how much folic acid each of these foods contains. In addition, tell your readers that most multivitamins contain folic acid. Use a similar method in choosing the content needed to answer the other questions.

Organizing Your Content

When *organizing* your content, as when *choosing* it, keep your readers' needs firmly in mind. In the HMO example, the questions raised suggest that the brochure will be issue or topic oriented. That is, it will give information about specific topics within the general subject of folic acid and neural tube malformations. Many informative reports present a major topic divided into several subtopics, like this:

Topic	Exposure to insecticides
Subtopic 1	Exposure through food
Subtopic 2	Exposure through water
Subtopic 3	Exposure through air
and so on	

In the HMO example, the answers to the questions will be the topics and subtopics for the brochure. How to arrange them still needs to be decided. Your audience analysis told you that most of your readers will not know what neural tube birth malformations are. This suggests that you should first define the term. Definitions grow out of the scheme for a logical definition:

term = genus or class + differentia

In other words, begin your definition by identifying what general class or category your subject belongs to and then provide details to fine-tune your description. For example:

Neural tube malformations are serious birth defects that cause disability or death. They are the most common disabling birth defects, affecting between 1 and 2 out of every 1,000 births in the United States.

There are two main kinds of neural tube malformations: anencephaly and spina bifida. A baby with anencephaly does not develop a brain and dies shortly after birth. Spina bifida is a malformation of the spinal column. If the vertebrae (i.e., bones of the spinal column) surrounding the spinal cord do not close properly during the first 28 days of fetal development, the cord or spinal fluid will bulge through, usually in the lower back.[1]

Look at the first sentence, which follows the scheme for a logical definition:

Neural tube malformations *(term)* are serious birth defects *(genus)* that cause disability or death *(differentia)*.

This definition is then extended with additional information, such as statistics and descriptions; graphic illustrations could be added as well. Remember, however, that you should not add more detail than your purpose and your readers' needs require.

After you have told your readers what neural tube malformations are, what do you do next? Look at your questions again:

What are neural tube malformations?

Will folic acid prevent neural tube malformations?

How much folic acid is required?

When do I need to take folic acid?

Why are neural tube malformations dangerous?

Who is in danger?

What foods or food supplements will provide a sufficient supply of folic acid?

Next, it would seem to be a good idea to emphasize just how dangerous spina bifida is and who is in danger by describing some of the disabilities involved and adding some graphic illustrations. After you have made a convincing case regarding the dangers of spina bifida, you could then answer the questions concerning folic acid as a preventive measure that all women of childbearing age should follow. The questions concerning folic acid would lend themselves to being organized as a series of subtopics under one topic, like this:

> Will folic acid prevent neural tube malformations?
>> When do I need to take folic acid?
>> How much folic acid is required?
>> What foods or food supplements will provide a sufficient supply of folic acid?

Laypeople follow topical discussions well if you use the questions that generated the topics as your organizing device and the actual questions as topic headings. Therefore, your final organizational outline for the brochure might look like this:

> What are neural tube malformations?
> Why are neural tube malformations dangerous?
> Will folic acid prevent neural tube malformations?
>> When do I need to take folic acid?
>> How much folic acid is required?
>> What foods or food supplements will provide a sufficient supply of folic acid?

Although every topical organizational plan grows out of answers to questions, you need not use questions as headings in every situation. For example, for a more expert audience, question-type headings might be inappropriate.

You have many organizational schemes available. You may use one of them to organize your entire report and others to organize sections or even paragraphs within it. Here, briefly explained, are some of the most common organizational schemes.

Chronological

In a *chronological* scheme, information is organized by time. Choose this scheme to report a sequence of events or explain the steps in a process.

The following example shows a sequence of events in the order in which they happened:

Event 1	The accident
Event 2	The investigation
Event 3	The trial
and so on	

Chronology is also a major organizing pattern in process descriptions:

Step 1	Design the product
Step 2	Build the prototype
Step 3	Test the prototype

Classification and Division

In *classification,* you work from the specific to the general, seeking classifications (that is, categories) for items. For example, your knowledge of house windows might tell you that their frames are made of various materials, such as aluminum, wood, vinyl, and fiberglass. Therefore, in writing about windows, you might find it convenient to classify them by their framing materials. In *division,* you work from the general to the specific. That is, you might start with the generalization *house windows* and divide by *framing materials.*

Whether you start at the bottom with specifics or at the top with a generalization, the result is the same: a classification and a set of items that belong in it. For example:

House windows
    Aluminum
    Wood
    Vinyl
    Fiberglass

Be sure that every equal classification or division is based on the same principle. That is, in a classification scheme based on window frame materials, do not introduce another equal classification based on durability. It would be appropriate, however, to create subclassifications based on features such as durability, cost, and efficiency:

House windows

    Aluminum

        Durability

        Cost

        Efficiency

Keep your purpose and audience in mind when choosing a classification scheme. For instance, suppose you are classifying *insecticides*. For chemists, it might be most appropriate to classify insecticides by their chemical properties; however, for farmers, it might be best to classify according to the types of insects the insecticides control. You could classify *cities* in literally thousands of ways: by location; racial/ethnic mix; population; numbers of hotels and restaurants; type of government; availability, number, and size of convention rooms; and so forth. For convention planners, classification schemes based on the numbers of restaurants, hotels, and convention rooms might best serve their interests.

Mechanism Descriptions

Descriptions of mechanisms are common in technical writing. You will find many examples in technical advertisements, empirical research reports, and instructions. As always, the amount of detail presented should be based on your purpose, your readers' concerns and characteristics, your readers' level of knowledge and experience in the area, and your readers' attitudes toward your purpose. But in general, mechanism descriptions follow a three-part scheme. Here is an example, explaining a mechanism called a *scarifier*, which is used to prepare forest floors for the regeneration of trees:

1. Overview	The modified drag-chain is designed to be pulled by crawler-tractors in the 30- to 50-horsepower class. The modified drag-chain scarifier was designed to expose mineral soil in spot areas under standing trees. Preliminary tests indicate

	that the modified chain may distribute seed better than rakes or disks, although rakes and disks may provide better soil disturbance.
2. Division into component parts and description of the parts	The modified drag-chain employs two lengths of lightweight drag-chain instead of the three heavy strands in the original. Two-inch-square bar stock, 24 inches long, welded to each length of chain, increases scarification. . . .
3. Mechanism in action	The chain is self-cleaning and rolls over slash downfall better than other implements. Roots of competing grasses are pulled out by the chain. . . .[2]

Mechanism descriptions are generally accompanied by graphic illustrations, such as drawings and photographs (discussed further in Chapter 6).

Because such situations occur so often in technical writing, many useful formats and organizational plans have been developed. You can often use these plans and formats, perhaps in modified form, to choose and organize content in your writing. Part Two, The Formats of Technical Writing, provides useful information on choosing and organizing content. Chapter 9, in particular, on formats of reports, gives detailed accounts of how to write instructions, analytical reports, proposals, progress reports, and empirical research reports.

Knowing the basic formats and uses of these organizational schemes will help you organize a piece of writing. But nothing is as important as choosing your content and organizing it around your purpose and audience. In the HMO brochure example, knowledge of your purpose and audience should have led you to organize your writing by topic, even if you had never heard of topical arrangement.

Outlines

Make an outline when you are organizing. Writing ideas down helps clarify your thoughts. Ideas not written down may be forgotten. If you are trying to write something down and you are not able to express it clearly, you may be taking the wrong approach. You do not necessarily need to make a formal outline full of roman numerals and capital letters. But you should keep a good record of your organization with an informal outline of headings and subheadings. When you have a coherent outline that matches your purpose and audience, you will be ready to write.

Should you need a formal outline, carefully follow the format in Figure 3.1, which illustrates a typical topic outline. In outlines, the letters and numbers that serve as labels alternate, like this:

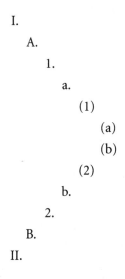

Notice that the logic of an outline requires that you have a *II* when you have a *I*, a *B* when you have an *A*, and so on through the outline. As in Figure 3.1, begin your outline with a statement that clearly indicates your purpose and audience.

Solar Water Heating

Before considering installing a solar water heater, homeowners should understand the components and types of solar water heaters currently available, estimate the size of the system they need, and consider the economic and environmental benefits of installed systems.

I. Solar water heater components
   A. Collectors
      1. Flat-plate collectors
      2. Evacuated-tube collectors
      3. Concentrating collectors
   B. Storage tanks
   C. Pumps
II. Types of solar water heaters
   A. Active systems
      1. Open-loop systems
         a. Advantages
         b. Disadvantages
      2. Closed-loop systems
         a. Advantages
         b. Disadvantages
   B. Passive systems
      1. Batch heaters
         a. Advantages
         b. Disadvantages
      2. Thermosiphon systems
         a. Advantages
         b. Disadvantages
III. System size
IV. Benefits of solar water heaters
   A. Economic benefits
      1. Florida Solar Energy Center analysis
      2. Paybacks
   B. Environmental benefits

FIGURE 3.1   Topic Outline

Source: Adapted from *Solar Water Heating* (Washington, DC: U.S. Department of Energy, 1996).

ACTIVITIES

1. Use the Internet to locate at least two articles on evaluating Internet sources. Analyze the articles to determine if they are credible sources. If not, continue to search until you have identified two sources. Share what you learn about evaluating sources with your classmates, and explain how you determined that these were credible sources.

2. Bring a short example of technical writing (for example, a letter, a brochure, a flyer, a quick reference sheet) and outline its content. In addition to outlining its content, identify the organization scheme or schemes the author used. Do you think this scheme is helpful to the intended audience? Why or why not?

CHAPTER ASSIGNMENTS

Assignment 1 for Individual Writers: The Analytical Report

Your assignment for this chapter requires you to conduct secondary research on the Internet. Your research should focus on the following questions your supervisor has asked you to answer:

1. What is groupware or Web-based collaborative software?

2. What are the most popular groupware products?

3. What are the features of the most popular groupware products?

4. What do these features allow users to do, or what kinds of tasks can groups complete with these products?

To answer these questions, you will probably need to start with a good search engine that will help you locate resources, including definitions and product descriptions of groupware. When you find these resources, you may print copies that contain information relevant to your report, or you may decide to simply take notes. However you decide to gather your information, always identify the location of the information, so you can return to the page if necessary. When you have finished your research, sort through the information and organize it, choosing specific organization schemes. Create an outline that illustrates how you will answer your supervisor's questions in your report.

After you have outlined your report, you may want to compare your outline with those of other writers in your class. Reviewing your writing plan and outline with others is a good way to identify weaknesses in your plan and to correct them before you begin to write. When your outline is as clearly organized as possible, write the first draft of your report.

Assignment 2 for a Writing Team: The Recommendation Report

Your assignment for this chapter requires you to conduct additional Internet research. Before you begin your research, you and your teammates will need to compare notes from your analytical reports and identify the groupware products you think are the best candidates for your company. Take notes on why you think these are the best products to research.

After you have identified three to five of the best products, you will need to research them more thoroughly to see how well they meet your company's criteria: an inexpensive or free application that allows workers to write collaboratively, share files, access calendars and other project management tools, and communicate with instant messaging or e-mail. The groupware application should also be easy to use. If possible, download free trials of the groupware and see how well they work.

Take notes on all your research, organize your notes, and create an outline that will answer your research question: Which of these products is best for your company?

Review your outline with your teammates and divide the writing among you. Write the first draft of your assigned section.

4

Write Clearly and Precisely

When you write the first draft of a document, do it rapidly and without much regard for mechanics and style. Using the content and organization you have arrived at (by following the guidelines in Chapters 1–3), get your information out where you can see it. Writing is thinking, so often while writing you will see different ways of organizing and different content choices. Follow the flow of your writing. Don't be a slave to organizational plans.

When you have completed your first draft, it is time to make sure that your paragraphing, sentence structure, and language present your content clearly and precisely. This chapter will help you to revise your draft to meet your readers' needs. The first half of the chapter will provide you with recommendations for revising the components that make up your draft. The second half discusses steps you should take to check your revisions, and it provides you with strategies for revising drafts created in teams.

Paragraph for Readers

Imagine reading page after page of prose without any paragraphs. They would appear dense and forbidding. Therefore, the first principle of paragraphing is to *paragraph often*, so you don't intimidate your readers. Judging by standard practice in well-written prose, paragraphs of 60 to

100 words seem about right, depending in part on the page design. For example, letters or pages that are formatted in narrow columns will likely have shorter paragraphs than standard report pages.

In technical writing, the first sentence in a paragraph generally introduces its subject and frequently provides a transition from the previous paragraph. You don't need to be heavy handed about either the introduction or the transition. These few paragraphs illustrate how to introduce the topic in the first paragraph and then move on to subtopics in subsequent paragraphs:

> The three major causes of land degradation are destructive agricultural practices, deforestation, and overgrazing.
>
> Destructive agricultural practices and land mismanagement account for 27 percent of the world's soil degradation, much of it in North America. Soil has been lost by repeated use of conventional tillage with heavy equipment and failure to use contour plowing on sloping terrain. Since 1930, the U.S. Government has spent $18 billion in conservation measures to reduce soil erosion. Despite present expenditures of $1 billion a year, the U.S. still annually loses some 6 billion tons of topsoil.
>
> Land degradation is especially acute in the former Soviet Union, a consequence of short-sighted industrial agricultural practices that ignored natural factors and faith that technology, fertilizers, and pesticides could increase crop yields interminably. Of Russia's 13.6 million acres of irrigated land, one-fifth is too salinized and two-fifths too acidified to support production. . . .
>
> Deforestation exposes fragile tropical soils to rainfall. . . .
>
> Overgrazing causes 35 percent of desertification, the most prevalent type of soil degradation. . . .[1]

The first one-sentence paragraph serves as a transition from the previous subject by announcing that the new subject will be *the three major causes of land degradation.* The first sentence in the second paragraph makes the transition to *destructive agricultural practices in North America.* The rest of the paragraph provides supporting data.

The first sentence of the third paragraph lets you know that *land degradation* is still the subject but the focus has shifted to the former Soviet Union, and so on. The fourth paragraph, on *deforestation,* makes the transition to the new subject simply by beginning *Deforestation exposes. . . .*

The transition to *overgrazing* is made with the paragraph beginning *Overgrazing causes. . . .*

The writer shifts gears between subjects simply by using key terms. The writer also keeps the reader's eyes on the subject by repeating key terms. Notice how many times *degradation* occurs in the sample paragraphs. (For that matter, notice how many times the words *paragraph* and *paragraphs* occur in this section discussing paragraphs.)

Not repeating key terms—or worse, using variant terms (for example, *deterioration* for *degradation*)—may cause your readers to lose sight of the subject or to think that a shift in subject has occurred. Don't be afraid to use intelligent repetition.

Take a moment now to look at your draft to see if you have used these strategies in your paragraphs. Do you use transitions in the first sentence to connect a new paragraph to the previous one? Do you announce the subject of the paragraph in the first or second sentence? Do you use key terms or synonyms to make connections between paragraphs and within paragraphs? If not, revise your paragraphs to make them better connected to each other. If you do so, your readers will appreciate how easy it is to follow the train of thought from one idea to the next in your document.

Revise Sentences and Words for Readers

The next series of guidelines offers you suggestions for revising your sentences and words to make them more readable and understandable for readers. After you read *each* section, take a moment to review your current draft. Check it to see if you can revise it using the suggestion presented in the section. Reading the draft repeatedly, thinking about these guidelines one section at a time and working on improvements, will take time at first, but doing so can help you build the skills you need to revise your documents to make them more reader-friendly.

Think of this practice as if you were training for a marathon. No one trains for a marathon by running 26 miles the first day. You must start out gradually, adding miles over weeks of training until you reach marathon distance. Learning to revise is a similar process. Train yourself to revise quickly by taking your time now, playing close attention to each suggestion as you implement it. Before you know it, you will be able to revise sentences and words using many guidelines at once, but that will happen only after you gain skill slowly over time.

Use Language Appropriate for Your Readers

When you have done your audience analysis, you should have a good idea of the language level you can use. For instance, you will not want to throw terms from physics, sociology, or agronomy at readers who are not knowledgeable in those fields. On the other hand, for experts in these areas, more sophisticated language would be appropriate and even expected.

Here, for example, are a few sentences aimed at readers who are presumed to be knowledgeable about the words and concepts of molecular biophysics. For the intended audience, the language used is entirely appropriate. For other readers, however, at least several of the words and concepts presented will cause difficulty:

> To what degree do the mechanics of soluble protein motions apply to membrane proteins? Helices in membrane proteins are believed to be as tightly packed as those in soluble proteins. This crucial fact, which implies that the constraints on soluble proteins also apply to membrane proteins, is borne out by calculations showing that the buried atoms in membrane proteins occupy the same (or even less) space as comparable atoms in soluble proteins.[2]

Notice the difference in the language used in the next example, which is from a publication of the American Heart Association. This text is clearly aimed at intelligent but uninformed readers:

> When a heart attack occurs, the dying part of the heart may trigger electrical activity that causes *ventricular fibrillation*. This is an uncoordinated twitching of the ventricles that replaces the smooth, measured contractions that pump blood to the body's organs. Many times if trained medical professionals are immediately available, they can use electrical shock to start the heart beating again.
>
> If the heart can be kept beating and the heart muscle is not too damaged, small blood vessels may gradually reroute blood around blocked arteries. This is how the heart compensates; it's called *collateral circulation*.

For the most part, the American Heart Association sample uses simple, everyday words, such as *trigger, twitch,* and *blocked.* The two technical terms used—*ventricular fibrillation* and *collateral circulation*—are well-defined.

Inflated language is never appropriate for any audience. Resist the temptation to impress your readers with fancy and pompous words. Choose simple, common words as much as possible. Don't *utilize* things; *use* them. Don't *initiate* and *terminate* things; *start* and *stop* them. Avoid phrases like *due to the fact that* and *at the present time;* simple words like *because* and *now* will serve you and your readers better.

Prefer the Active Voice

Active-voice sentences clearly state who or what the actor is and what the actor is doing. For that reason, most readers find sentences written in the active voice easier to follow and understand than those written in the passive voice. In addition, sentences written in the active voice seem more direct and interesting. You should use the active voice for the bulk of your writing.

In active-voice sentences, the subject acts in some way. For example:

The director reported that the spacecraft will begin mapping operations earlier than expected.

Phase I of the program runs until June.

The proposal includes two missions for 2010.

Notice that the subject does not have to be a person. As shown in these examples, the subject can be a *phase,* a *proposal*—anything at all.

In a passive-voice sentence, the subject is acted upon:

The ultraviolet emissions were detected by several astronomers.

Satellites, such as the earth's moon, are bound to their planets by the pull of gravity.

It is all too easy in a passive-voice sentence to omit the final prepositional phrase (beginning with *by*) that identifies the actor, even when that knowledge may be important. For example:

New technology was developed to revolutionize high-speed air travel.

Rewriting this sentence in the active voice requires adding an actor—who or what developed the new technology:

NASA developed new technology to revolutionize high-speed air travel.

Passive voice does have a place. When the identity of the actor is obvious or irrelevant (as is often the case in the Materials and Methods section of a research report), use the passive voice:

> Relative air moisture (percent) in the tunnel house was recorded using 2 HMP35C probes (Campbell Scientific) installed 2 m (6.6 ft) from the soil. A data logging system (Campbell Scientific Model CR-10) was programmed to compile data obtained from a probe every 5 minutes and to calculate hourly averages. Mean daily and monthly moisture levels were determined by a program developed using SAS software.[3]

Use the passive voice when it is appropriate, but prefer the active voice on most occasions. Your readers will appreciate it.

Use Personal Pronouns

Personal pronouns go hand in hand with the active voice. If the author or authors of a report wish to express an opinion or relate an action, it would be appropriate to write an active-voice sentence that begins with *I* or *we,* as in:

> I recommend the opening of the new office in Dayton as soon as possible.

Not to use *I* in this sentence would result in a lifeless passive-voice sentence:

> The opening of a new office in Dayton is recommended by the author.

The following would be even worse, because now no one is accepting responsibility for the recommendation:

> The opening of a new office in Dayton is recommended.

Using the personal pronoun *you* in instructions clarifies the actor and personalizes the instructions, as in this passage from Internal Revenue Service (IRS) tax instructions:

> You can deduct the actual cost of running your car or truck or take the standard mileage rate. You must use actual costs if you do not own the vehicle or if you used more than one vehicle simultaneously (such as in fleet operations).

Take away the use of *you,* and the result would likely be the impersonal passive voice, harder to read and understand and vague about who is doing what:

> The actual cost of running a car or truck can be deducted or the standard mileage rate can be used. Actual costs must be used if the vehicle is not owned or if more than one vehicle is used simultaneously (such as in fleet operations).

In tax instructions, the IRS refers to itself as *we,* as in:

> If you want, we will figure the tax for you.

The use of *we* in instructions is appropriate, as long as it is clear who *we* is. In the previous example, the use of *IRS* would have worked about as well as *we.* But *we* sounds much more friendly and personal, which may have a positive effect on the audience.

Often, you would be wise to make clear the *references* of your terms at the beginning of your instructions. For example, at the beginning of an insurance policy, you might note that *we* refers to the insurance company and *you* refers to the policyholder.

Use Action Verbs

Using action verbs is closely related to using active voice and personal pronouns. All these style decisions help you avoid using *nominalizations,* which are nouns derived from verbs. For example, *instruction* comes from *instruct,* and *assessment* comes from *assess.*

There is nothing wrong with using nominalizations, as long as they are used properly. Using *instructions* in a sentence like this is fine, for example:

> Computer companies have learned that good instructions sell computers.

But you would be on soft ground and sinking fast if you wrote this passage in a letter to an office manager:

> Misuse of the computer network by your secretaries has become evident. Please make provision for your secretaries to receive proper instruction in the use of the network.

This passage is stuffy, wordy, and not specific. This rewrite is better:

> Your secretaries are misusing the computer network with personal mail. Please instruct them to use the network for business mail only.

In the revised passage, the writer uses action verbs and specifies what the problem actually is.

Unfortunately, you will find a good many nominalizations in technical writing, such as this one:

> The emission of sulfur dioxide from the factory is much greater than the emission of hydrogen sulfide.

If you find such a clumsy sentence in your work, think about where the action is and rewrite the sentence with an action verb:

> The factory emits much more sulfur dioxide than hydrogen sulfide.

When you are revising your work, look out for nominalizations. Better still, use the Find or Search function of your computer. Look for words that end in *-ment, -ion, -ance, -ence, -al,* and *-ing.* If you find any nominalizations, check to see if you have used them properly. If you have not, revise them by using action verbs.

Don't Introduce Unnecessary Complication

Both research and intuition will tell you that the more highly educated readers are, the more sentence complexity they can tolerate. But *no* readers appreciate sentences that are too long or tortured.

Think Subject-Verb The subject and verb of a sentence are its frame, upon which you can hang various grammatical segments to expand or clarify the information provided by the subject and verb. To illustrate this process, here are a few examples:

> OPEC could easily produce half of all the oil consumed in the world.
>
> By 2010, OPEC could easily produce half of all the oil produced in the world.
>
> Because OPEC members control such a huge share of the world's high-quality, low-cost oil reserves, by 2010, OPEC could easily produce half of all the oil produced in the world.

None of these sentences should cause difficulty for a reader with at least high school reading ability. In all of them, the basic subject-verb frame stays clearly in view. The added grammatical segments provide additional information but do not excessively complicate matters.

Use a Reasonable Sentence Length What is a *reasonable* sentence length? The answer to this question obviously relates closely to the abilities of your readers. Most high school graduates can read longer sentences than elementary schoolchildren, and most college-educated readers can read longer sentences than high school students. Moreover, readers familiar with the subject under discussion can read longer sentences than those who are not.

As shown by the examples in the last section, sentences grow in length as information is added to them. At some point, they can be too long and too complicated, regardless of readers' abilities. The sentence in this example is probably too long for most readers:

> Because of OPEC members', especially the Persian Gulf members', control over such a huge share of the world's high-quality, low-cost oil reserves, the willingness and ability of OPEC members to expand production capacity, including production potential from Kuwait and Iraq, and the limited ability of non-OPEC producers to expand production facilities, by 2010, OPEC could easily produce half of all the oil produced in the world, which will greatly influence prospects for world oil prices.

A reader's ability to handle long, complicated sentences relates not only to the reader's own skill but also to the skill with which the writer constructs sentences. Therefore, it is risky to set limits on sentence length. It seems clear, however, that sentences that exceed 40 or 50 words are too difficult for most people. Professional writers average about 20 words a sentence. That average is likely one that most writers should strive for.

Write Positively Too many negative words in a sentence can cause unnecessary complication, particularly in instructions. The problem occurs when negative words—such as *no, none,* and *not*—are combined with words that begin with negative prefixes—such as *ir-* (*irrelevant*), *non-* (*noncommittal*), and *un-* (*unbroken*). For example, the first sentence that follows is more difficult to read than the second:

> The virus protection is not installed properly until the virus protection icon appears at the bottom of your screen.

> The virus protection is installed properly when the virus protection icon appears at the bottom of your screen.

In reading the first sentence, readers will have a momentary pause while translating the negative combination *not . . . until* into a positive statement. The second sentence, already written positively, presents no such complication.

Avoid Long Noun Strings   Using nouns to modify other nouns is commonplace in English. Expressions like *mail carrier* and *consumption level* are grammatically correct and understandable. But using long noun strings to modify other nouns introduces complications that raise difficulties for the reader, as in this example:

> Surplus production energy capacity price fluctuation control policies seem doomed to failure.

Policies is the word modified by the long noun string. That much is clear, but little else is. In the seven-word modifying phrase, the reader has to pause and sort out which words or groups of words modify other words or groups of words. The writer should do the sorting, perhaps in this way:

> The policies for controlling price fluctuations caused by surplus production in energy capacity seem doomed to failure.

Review your own writing to identify noun strings. Be wary if you see that you have put together more than three nouns to modify another noun without using clarifying hyphens or prepositions. You probably need to rewrite the sentence.

Check for Parallelism   Write parallel ideas in parallel grammatical form. In this well-written sentence, the writer uses parallelism to good effect:

> Storms, floods, droughts, and fires that accompanied the unusually strong El Niño of 1997–1998 took more than 30,000 lives, displaced about a third of a billion people, and in less than a year ran up a tab of nearly 100 billion dollars in material damages.[4]

The three parallel verbs—*took, displaced,* and *ran up*—tie together the clauses of a fairly long sentence, making it easy to read despite its length.

In the next example, the writer starts the list of symptoms with two noun phrases, switches to an infinitive phrase, and ends with a dependent clause:

> Signs of a heart attack include a sensation of fullness, pain in the center of the chest, to faint, and when you feel a shortness of breath.

You really don't have to know all that grammatical terminology to recognize that this sentence has gone wrong somehow. It has become complicated and more difficult to understand than it should be. Fix the sentence by putting all the symptoms in the same grammatical form:

> Signs of a heart attack are a sensation of fullness, pain in the center of the chest, fainting, and shortness of breath.

When making a list, take care to keep all the elements of the list in parallel grammatical form, as the writer does in this example:

> Short-term climate anomalies, such as we experienced with El Niño, can serve as analogs for what might happen in the course of future global greenhouse warming. Some of the relevant impacts of the 1997–98 El Niño are listed below:
>
> - A rise of about six inches in sea level along the coast of California.
> - Substantially higher than normal temperatures over land.
> - Changes in precipitation patterns, leading to flooding in some areas (such as Chile, Peru, California, and the southeastern U.S.).[5]

The writer kept his list parallel by using noun phrases based on *rise, temperatures,* and *changes.* Also, the use of bullets (·) helps clarify and organize the list for readers.

Writing and Revising with Others

When you have completed your first draft and revised it using this chapter's suggested guidelines, it is a good idea, especially if you are writing alone, to share it with an editor, a fellow writer, or, even better, one of your identified readers. Ask this individual to read your draft, check it for accuracy and completeness, and suggest ideas for revision. Then revise again, if necessary, to incorporate your reader's suggestions.

If you are writing with others, your team will need to combine your revised individual sections into a common document. You can use several strategies to combine your sections into one document, but to begin, you will need access to each file. If everyone on your team is in the same location, you can save all files onto a common storage device or computer drive. You have several options for creating the common document once you have all the files in one location. The easiest method is to open each document in your word processor, and then copy and paste each writer's section into one file. This technique is quick and simple, but it can cause formatting problems if your team has not established common margins and formatting guidelines beforehand. Another simple strategy is to use your word processor's Insert → File command. To begin, open the first section of the paper; then insert the remaining files into the first section in the order you want them to appear in your document.

If team members are in different locations, each member can e-mail attached files to a designated member who will combine them into one document. Another option for teams working at a distance is to use a collaborative writing application, or groupware, such as Google Docs or Adobe's Buzzword. Groupware allows you to upload sections, combine them, and revise them online. Then you can edit, download, and finally print the file, just like you would with a word processor. Wikis are another Internet option for writing and editing in groups. Wikis allow group members to upload and revise together, but a wiki is best for creating Web pages, so if you are creating a print document, another strategy would probably work best.

Whichever strategy you use for combining your files into a single document, you will need to assign or designate a team member to read, review, and revise the combined document draft to make certain it is complete. That team member will also need to check that everyone has used words, paragraphs, headings, and other components consistently. It may also be necessary to reformat all sections of the document to make margins and headings consistent. (Chapter 5 provides suggestions for designing and formatting your draft.)

Finally, after you have thoroughly edited your draft for consistency, conduct a final review of your document to check for completeness and accuracy. For example, ask an SME (subject matter expert) to read the document. Another effective strategy is to have actual readers or users review or test the document to see if it contains all the information they need to complete the instructions or take an action. Reviews like these will provide your team with valuable information that ensures your document is readable and useful after it is published.

ACTIVITIES

1. Work with a partner to critique a short technical writing sample and recommend changes to it. Begin your critique by describing how the writer has used paragraphs, sentences, and specific words. (Try to describe what the writer has done using the language or terms from this chapter.) After reviewing the sample, determine whether the writer has effectively applied the guidelines described in this chapter. If so, where and how has the writer applied these guidelines? (Support your claims with evidence from the sample.) If not, how would you suggest the writer edit the sample's paragraphs, sentences, and word choices to improve them?

2. Use a sample of your own writing to see whether you can improve it using the guidelines described in this chapter. You might choose a sample you created from one of the activities in the previous chapters, or you can use a sample you have written for another purpose. Identify paragraphs, sentences, and word choices in your sample that could be improved. Using the language from this chapter to describe your writing, explain why these selections need revision and then revise them.

CHAPTER ASSIGNMENTS

Assignment 1 for Individual Writers: The Analytical Report

At this point, you should have a draft of your report written. Exchange your draft with one or two other writers in your class, and review each other's writing.

Begin your review by checking the draft for content. Does the report respond to the audience's needs by answering the following questions:

1. What is groupware or Web-based collaborative software?

2. What are the most popular groupware products?

3. What are the features of the most popular groupware products?

4. What do these features allow users to do, or what kinds of tasks can groups complete with these products?

If the questions are adequately answered, tell the writer. If not, identify the questions that are not well answered.

After you have reviewed the draft for content, check it for effective use of paragraphs, sentences, and word choices. Start by identifying strengths in the draft and tell the writer what he or she is doing correctly in these locations. Then reread the draft, looking for weaknesses. Explain to the writer what weaknesses you have found, and suggest revisions that would strengthen these weaknesses. Use the language in this chapter to describe what you see as strengths and weaknesses. Share your comments with the writer and suggest revisions.

Assignment 2 for a Writing Team: The Recommendation Report

By now, each member of your group should have drafted his or her section of your report. At the end of this chapter, your group must complete two tasks: (1) create a combined document, and (2) review and edit the combined document to make sure it is consistent from one section to the next. Begin this work by combining all of your sections into a working draft, using the guidelines in this chapter. When you have a complete draft, you are ready to review the different sections. Some groups choose a single writer to read and review the combined draft and make it consistent. Other groups cycle the document through several readers. Your group should decide how you want to review your document and then conduct the review. No matter what decision you make, you should always ask a second reader to make a final pass through the document to check it for consistent use of paragraphs, sentences, and word choices throughout.

5

Use Good Page Design

Well-designed pages increase the accessibility of your report by helping readers see its organization. By making your presentation visually attractive, good design increases the likelihood that your audience will read carefully.

Good page design also allows your readers to access the information that is most important to them. For example, imagine that you are writing a recommendation report to help your supervisor decide which service plan to choose for your organization's mobile phones. After you have submitted the report, your supervisor may read the entire report closely, checking criteria for phone service and comparing features. But your supervisor will probably need to get approval before purchasing the service plan. To get this approval, several other readers will need to review the report. The manager above your supervisor will likely only read the executive summary at the front of the report, but the company accountant will want to focus on basic charges, fees, and other expenses found in the budget. Careful page design and layout will help these readers find the information most important to them.

Elements of good design that help readers access information include headings, headers and footers, appropriate type size and typeface, lists and informal tables, discreet typographical emphasis, and the ample use of white space. Most of the suggestions in this chapter are effective for both print and electronic documents. When the suggestions vary for print or electronic documents, the section provides separate recommendations.

Use Default Layout Templates Cautiously

Many word-processing, electronic slide show, and desktop publishing software applications include default layouts or templates for preparing documents such as letters, memos, reports, and slide shows. These software packages include "wizards"—easy step-by-step instructions—for inserting your information into templates. Because these templates are so easy to use, many beginning writers rely on them to design and lay out their documents. While templates are easy to use, they are not always appropriate for your particular audience and their communication needs. Templates may include unnecessary headings, incorporate distracting visuals, and require information that is unnecessary for your purpose. That is the bad news.

The good news is that most of these templates are modifiable, so you can change them to fit your writing situation. A good strategy for deciding whether to use a template or not is to compare the default templates with similar documents created in your organization. Change the template to fit your content, organization, and overall communication purpose and needs. You can make these changes by deleting unnecessary components of the template and adding other components that your document requires.

The following sections provide you with guidelines for using page design elements that most technical communication documents include.

Provide Headings

The use of headings reduces the density of type on the page and provides easy transitions from one topic to the next. Mainly, headings make information more accessible to readers because they allow readers to scan content quickly to find what they need.

Different levels of headings identify topics and subtopics within a document, making its organization clear to readers. By scanning headings or using them in conjunction with a matching table of contents (see p. 107), readers can find the sections they need or want to read. For example, an accountant reading a report about a new financial spreadsheet may be most interested in the how-to instructions. The accountant's boss, however, may be most interested in how the new spreadsheet may make the accountant more efficient.

Compare Figures 5.1 and 5.2 to see what a difference in readability a few well-placed headings can make.

Because the main role of headings is to increase accessibility, do not use more than three or four levels of headings. Too many headings chop

---

At present, USGS investigates three types of severe coastal storm impacts: hurricanes in the southeast U.S., extra-tropical storm impacts on the U.S. west coast during El-Niño, and "northeaster" impacts on the U.S. east coast.

Hurricanes are tropical storms that have a sustained wind speed greater than 75MPH. In the northern hemisphere, these low pressure systems rotate counterclockwise. As a hurricane approaches the coast, the wind speed on the right side of the storm is added to the forward speed of the storm. Hence, the greatest impacts from storm surge, wave battering and wind speed tend to occur to the right of the eye at landfall. Storm surge is an increase in sea level along the coast caused primarily by strong onshore winds and low barometric pressure. The strongest hurricanes are Category 5, having sustained wind speeds in excess of 155MPH and storm surge in excess of 6 m (20 ft). In recorded history, only two Category 5 hurricanes have made landfall in the United States.

During severe El-Niño, the jet stream over the Pacific Ocean tends to be more southerly than normal, guiding winter extra-tropical storms into California and bringing extensive rainfall and large waves to the California coast. During the severe El-Niños of 1982-83 and 1997-98 extensive coastal erosion and damage occurred along the west coast. Under El-Niño conditions of equatorial warming in the Pacific, hurricanes are less frequent in the north Atlantic. The reoccurrence of La-Niña, equatorial cooling in the Pacific, coincides with active hurricane seasons for the southeast United States.

Northeasters, or winter extra-tropical storms impacting the east coast of the United States, can cause considerable coastal change and damage. For example, one of the most destructive storms to ever impact the mid-Atlantic states was the Ash Wednesday storm of 1962. Extensive coastal change occurred over 1,000 km of coast. Northeasters owe their destructive power to their long duration. Winds are typically below hurricane force, but can persist for several days to a week, generating large waves and enhanced storm surge. In comparison, hurricanes are more severe in terms of wind speed and storm surge but the shoreline impacts tend to be more localized, confined to order 100 km of coast. Hurricanes also tend to be more short-lived, moving across coastal areas in hours rather than days.

FIGURE 5.1   Document Without Headings

Source: Adapted from U.S. Geological Survey, *Hurricanes and Extreme Storm Impact Studies,* http://www.wvdhsem.gov/WV_Disaster_Library/Library/Hurricanes/ Hurricane%20and%20Extreme%20Storm%20Impact%20Studies.htm (Accessed June 3, 2009).

Hurricane and Extreme Storm Impact Studies
Hurricanes, El-Niño, & Northeasters—An Introduction

At present, USGS investigates three types of severe coastal storm impacts: hurricanes in the southeast U.S., extra-tropical storm impacts on the U.S. west coast during El-Niño, and "northeaster" impacts on the U.S. east coast.

HURRICANES

Hurricanes are tropical storms that have a sustained wind speed greater than 75MPH. In the northern hemisphere, these low pressure systems rotate counterclockwise. As a hurricane approaches the coast, the wind speed on the right side of the storm is added to the forward speed of the storm. Hence, the greatest impacts from storm surge, wave battering and wind speed tend to occur to the right of the eye at landfall. Storm surge is an increase in sea level along the coast caused primarily by strong onshore winds and low barometric pressure. The strongest hurricanes are Category 5, having sustained wind speeds in excess of 155MPH and storm surge in excess of 6 m (20 ft). In recorded history, only two Category 5 hurricanes have made landfall in the United States.

EL-NIÑO

During severe El-Niño, the jet stream over the Pacific Ocean tends to be more southerly than normal, guiding winter extra-tropical storms into California and bringing extensive rainfall and large waves to the California coast. During the severe El-Niños of 1982-83 and 1997-98 extensive coastal erosion and damage occurred along the west coast. Under El-Niño conditions of equatorial warming in the Pacific, hurricanes are less frequent in the north Atlantic. The reoccurrence of La-Niña, equatorial cooling in the Pacific, coincides with active hurricane seasons for the southeast United States.

NORTHEASTERS

Northeasters, or winter extra-tropical storms impacting the east coast of the United States, can cause considerable coastal change and damage. For example, one of the most destructive storms to ever impact the mid-Atlantic states was the Ash Wednesday storm of 1962. Extensive coastal change occurred over 1,000 km of coast. Northeasters owe their destructive power to their long duration. Winds are typically below hurricane force, but can persist for several days to a week, generating large waves and enhanced storm surge. In comparison, hurricanes are more severe in terms of wind speed and storm surge but the shoreline impacts tend to be more localized, confined to order 100 km of coast. Hurricanes also tend to be more short-lived, moving across coastal areas in hours rather than days.

FIGURE 5.2   Document with Headings

Source: Adapted from U.S. Geological Survey, *Hurricanes and Extreme Storm Impact Studies*, http://www.wvdhsem.gov/WV_Disaster_Library/Library/Hurricanes/ Hurricane%20and%20Extreme%20Storm%20Impact%20Studies.htm (Accessed June 3, 2009).

a document into too many pieces and decrease, rather than increase, accessibility.

You will likely have two basic questions in using headings: (1) How do I phrase headings? and (2) How do I make headings noticeable and distinctive?

Phrasing Headings

Headings can be questions, short sentences, single words, or phrases of various types. For example, a document about government benefits might contain a section on qualifying for those benefits. The heading for this section could be phrased in various ways:

Who Can Qualify?

You May Qualify

Qualifications

Qualifying for Benefits

Questions seem to work well for headings, perhaps because they mirror what is in readers' minds. But the most important principle is that each heading should accurately identify what the section contains. For that reason, most headings should be substantive, rather than generic. A *generic* heading is a heading like "Part One," with no further identification. A generic heading such as "Introduction" or "Conclusion" serves the purpose adequately, but when used elsewhere in reports, generic headings do not give readers enough information. In the body of a report, use *substantive* headings that tell readers what they can expect to find in the sections, like these:

Biofilm Formation

Trends in Computer Use

Dangers of Self-Medication

Headings within any section of a document must be grammatically parallel (see pp. 43–44). For example, all the major topic headings must be parallel. The subtopic headings within a major section must also be parallel, but they do not have to be parallel to subtopic headings in other major sections. The Table of Contents for the two parts of this book makes this concept clear:

Part One	**The Seven Principles of Technical Writing**
1	Know Your Purpose and Your Writing Situation
2	Know Your Audience and Their Situation
3	Choose and Organize Your Content Around Your Purpose and Audience
4	Write Clearly and Precisely
5	Use Good Page Design
6	Think Visually
7	Write Ethically
Part Two	**The Formats of Technical Writing**
8	Elements of Reports
9	Formats of Reports
10	Formats of Correspondence

The headings for the two parts are parallel noun phrases. (They are also substantive.) The chapter headings in Part One are all active/imperative sentences. The headings in Part Two are all noun phrases: parallel with each other but not with the headings in Part One.

Making Headings Noticeable and Distinctive

Good choices of words and grammatical forms help make headings noticeable and distinctive. Beyond that, good choices of typographical formats for your headings make them noticeable and help to distinguish different levels of headings.

Figures 5.3 and 5.4 (pp. 54, 55) show some of the various types of headings available to you. Notice that distinctiveness is obtained through devices such as spacing, italicizing, capitalizing, centering, indenting, using different type sizes, and so forth. However, all these headings are in the same typeface. Using different typefaces for different headings may appear gimmicky.

You may also notice that underlining is rarely used anymore to emphasize headings or create emphasis on a page. Underlining was an effective way to create emphasis when documents were written on typewriters. Today, word processors allow you to use boldface, italics, and color to create emphasis. Underlining, especially on a Web page, makes words harder to read, so you should use underlining only if you have no other choices for emphasis.

When you are designing your pages, choose three or four of the available styles and stick with them throughout your document. Keep each heading with the section of text it identifies. Don't leave a heading dangling at the bottom of a page and start the section it identifies on the next page. Include at least two lines of the section's text with the heading. If you can't, move everything to the next page.

Use Headers and Footers

Headers and footers are other ways of keeping readers on track in a printed document. A *header* is a phrase that identifies the document or perhaps a section of it. As the name implies, a header appears at the head, or top, of the page. A *footer* contains the same basic information but appears at the foot, or bottom, of the page.

WRITE CLEARLY AND PRECISELY

USE GOOD PAGE DESIGN

Use Good Page Design

Write Clearly and Precisely

Use Good Page Design
  Write Clearly and Precisely
  Use good page design.

FIGURE 5.3   **Examples of Heading Styles**

In a short document, the title of the piece is usually presented in a header or footer. Sometimes, a header or footer may include the date and the name of the author of the document. In a longer document divided into chapters or major sections, the chapter or section heading is usually presented in a header or footer. Note that in this book, the part title is indicated on each left-hand page and the chapter title is indicated on each right-hand page.

Page numbers may appear with headers or footers or separately. Often, the information identifying the document or section will be in a header and the page number will be in a footer. Do not put an identifying header or footer on the title page or on the first pages of major sections, such as chapters. Do put page numbers on every page except the title page, however.

FRANCE

GEOGRAPHY
France is located

Boundaries
Bounded on the west by

Land Use
Although mostly flat plains

Arable land. About 33 percent of

Forest and woodland. About 27 percent of

POPULATION
The age structure of

GOVERNMENT
The French government is

FIGURE 5.4 Examples of Headings in Document

See Figure 5.5 for a selection of typical headers and footers.

Electronic documents also include headers and footers. Headers typically identify the Web site's owner and its content, including words and graphics that appear on all pages on the site. Subheadings may also be found below the identifying information to help readers immediately recognize what specific content the page contains. Web page footers typically include the last date on which the page was updated as well as links to the owner's e-mail address and other contact information.

Choose an Appropriate Type Size and Typeface

Deciding what is an *appropriate* type size and typeface most often means choosing type that eases the reader's task.

Type Size

Type sizes are expressed in units called *points.* The higher the number, or *point size*, the bigger the type:

9-point type

10-point type

12-point type

14-point type

18-point type

24-point type

In general, 10- to 12-point type is easy for most people to read in print documents. Use these sizes for the text in reports and correspondence. You may choose slightly larger type, such as 14-point, for headings to make them stand out from the text. Reserve type sizes from 18-point and up for brochures and other specialty items, for which you may want dramatic effects.

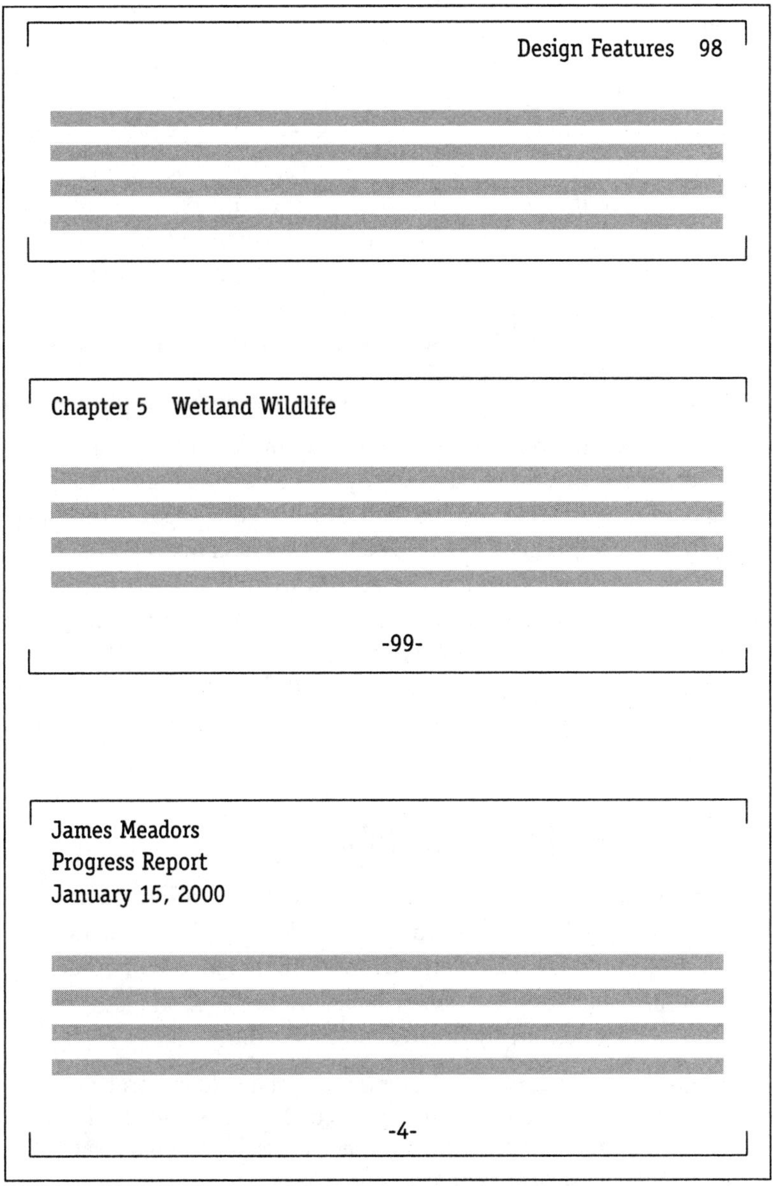

Design Features   98

Chapter 5   Wetland Wildlife

-99-

James Meadors
Progress Report
January 15, 2000

-4-

FIGURE 5.5   Typical Headers and Footers

Typeface

The two categories of type are *serif* and *sans serif. Serif* type has small extenders (called *serifs*) coming off the letters, as in the type used for most of the text in this book, which is Minion. Serifs help the eye connect letters in words and make recognizing words easier for readers of print documents. *Sans serif* type does not have these extenders, as in Helvetica type, which is used for some of the tables and figures in this book.

Conventional design wisdom says that serif type is easier to read and that sans serif type is more modern looking. As done in this book, serif type is generally used for large sections of text and sans serif type is frequently used for graphs and tables.

In electronic documents, designed for the Web or for electronic slide show presentations, sans serif fonts are more readable. Some sans serif fonts, such as Verdana and Georgia, are designed specifically for screen reading, and they are good choices when your pages are not text-heavy. If, however, your Web page is text-heavy, you may choose to use a serif font, like Times New Roman, for the text, but a sans serif font for headings. Whether you decide to use a sans serif font for both headings and text or a sans serif font for headings and serif for text, do not use more than two fonts per page. You can vary these font sizes on the page, but using more than two will make your page too busy for readers to scan easily.

Use Lists and Informal Tables

In both print and electronic documents, you can save words and open up your text by using lists and informal tables. Separate these elements from your text by indenting them at the left or both margins. Do not identify lists or informal tables with titles or table numbers.

A list with its accompanying text looks like this:

Steps to stop *Listeria* . . . *Listeria* is a common food-borne bacterium that can cause symptoms including nausea, vomiting, cramps, diarrhea and fever. To protect yourself and your family from *Listeria,* take these precautions:

- Thoroughly cook raw animal products.

- Thoroughly wash all food that is to be eaten raw, such as fruits and vegetables.

- Keep foods to be eaten raw separate from uncooked meats.

- Wash hands, knives and cutting boards with hot soapy water.

In addition, those most vulnerable to *Listeria* infections, such as pregnant women, the elderly, and those with weakened immune systems, also should . . . .[1]

Notice how bullets (•) are used to identify the list items. Numbers may also be used, but only if the order of the items in the list is important.

An informal table is essentially a list with columns (see Figure 5.6). Present informal tables as you do lists, but take care to align the separate columns of information. (See Chapter 6 for a discussion of formal tables.)

Use Emphasis Carefully

Use typographical variations to emphasize important points in your reports or correspondence. Variations include the following:

boldface

italic

larger type size

ALL CAPITAL LETTERS

When using any of these means of emphasis, be careful not to overdo it. A page with too many elements emphasized will look cluttered, and the

---

These five states have the largest projected net increases in immigrants, 1995 to 2025 (in millions):

California	8.8
New York	3.9
Florida	1.9
New Jersey	1.2
Illinois	1.0

States with lower projected increases: ▬▬▬▬▬▬▬▬
▬▬▬▬▬▬▬▬▬▬▬▬▬▬▬▬▬▬

FIGURE 5.6   An Informal Table

emphasis will be lost. Be particularly careful not to use all capital letters for more than one line. Because we rely on the ups and downs of capitals and lowercase letters in our reading, using all capitals raises the difficulty of reading. See Figure 5.7 for an example of typographical emphasis.

Leave Ample White Space

For ease of reading, a printed page should be about 50 percent type and 50 percent *white space* (a design term for "empty space"). Headings, lists, informal tables, and paragraphing all contribute to white space. In addition, you gain more white space with adequate margins, medium-length lines, and proper spacing. All measurements given here are based on using a standard 8-1/2" × 11" page.

Electronic pages need even more white space. For best readability, increase electronic page white space to 60 or 65 percent of the page.

Margins

Leave 1" for the top and side margins and 1–1/2" for the bottom margin. If you intend to bind your document, leave 1–1/2" to 2" on the side to be bound (usually the left).

Medium-Length Lines

Line length depends somewhat on the size and face of type used, but in most cases, a line of 50 to 70 characters (which is about 10 to 12 words) will be about right. In a double-column format, about 35 characters (or 5 words) per line is appropriate.

Should you *justify* your lines or not? That is, should your lines be even at both the left and right margins? Many word processors, in an attempt to justify the right margin, leave unattractive "rivers" of white space running through the text. Given this problem, you are better off in most instances to leave the right margin *ragged*—that is, unjustified. In any case, there seems to be little difference in readability between justified pages and ragged-right pages.

Proper Spacing

You have the choices of single-space, space-and-a-half, and double-space. Lines in memos and letters are traditionally single-spaced, with

Global Enterprises

DATE   15 September 2010

TO   Roy Goss
                    Ann Manchester
                    Jim Morris
                    Brittany Osborn
                    Al Smith

FROM   Pat Macintosh

SUBJECT   Schedule for Reporting Monthly Design Meetings

Thank you all for agreeing to report our monthly meetings. What follows is the schedule for the year:

2010		
October	Pat Macintosh	
November	Jim Morris	
December	Brittany Osborn	
2011		
January	Roy Goss	
February	Ann Manchester	
March	Al Smith	
April	Pat Macintosh	
May	Jim Morris	
June	Brittany Osborn	
July	Roy Goss	
August	Ann Manchester	
September	Al Smith	

If you can't report the month for which you are scheduled, call me and I'll arrange a switch. If I'm not available, call one of the other reporters listed to take your place.

Please use a memo format for your reports. Address them to Dave Buehler, and send copies to Sally Barker and me.

FIGURE 5.7   Example of Typographical Emphasis Within Memo

double-spacing between paragraphs. To achieve more white space in other documents, use space-and-a-half or double-spacing. Double-space the first draft of any document to allow room for corrections, changes, and scribbling.

ACTIVITIES

1. Practice using page layout terminology by describing the page layout features of this chapter. What features are present, and how are they used?

2. Examine the document templates available in your word-processing software. What kinds of templates are available? What features do the templates have? Are they modifiable? Modify and save at least two of the templates to learn how it is done.

CHAPTER ASSIGNMENTS

Assignment 1 for Individual Writers: The Analytical Report

This chapter provides guidelines for designing the pages of your report. Review the guidelines for report formats in Chapters 9 and 10, and then design your report in memo format to suit your audience's needs. Add headers or footers after page one as appropriate. Add other page layout features as needed to help your readers access the information you are providing. Review your work plan to make sure your page design reflects your readers' needs.

Assignment 2 for a Writing Team: The Recommendation Report

Your team's recommendation report is almost complete. Now you need to design its pages. Review the elements of formal reports in Chapter 8 before you begin this work. After you have identified the elements used in your recommendation report, design your report to help your readers access the information in it. You will need to insert headings, if you have not used them already, and decide how to indicate page order. Briefly work through the guidelines in this chapter to make sure you take advantage of all the page design strategies to make your report accessible and readable.

6

Think Visually

As you think about and plan your documents, think visually as well as verbally. Graphics of various kinds play a major role in technical writing, often presenting data and ideas more efficiently and precisely than words. In technical writing, you will use graphics to show objects, processes, and data. As you look at each sample graphic in this chapter, notice that the caption may be placed at either the bottom or top. Sometimes, the stylesheets for certain publications will dictate the placement of graphic captions. At other times, it will be your decision. In any case, be consistent with your placement throughout a document.

Getting and Showing Objects

The word *object* covers a lot of territory. It can mean a machine, mountain, tool, animal, pond, glacier, the inner ear—indeed, any material thing that you can see or feel. Photographs and drawings are used to portray objects.

Technical writing is frequently illustrated with objects like photographs, drawings, and other images. The Internet has made getting objects like these easy. For example, using a search engine, like Google's Image Search, you can locate objects that portray just about any subject. Yet objects, like texts, are copyrighted, so you must recognize and understand fair use laws before using them.

Unless photographs, illustrations, and clip art are designated as "free" or in the public domain, you must request permission from the image's creators or owners in order to use them. Even if the images are being used for educational purposes, you should read the guidelines for use before inserting them in a document, and you should follow the guidelines for use closely.

When you have permission to use objects, you still must document where you found them. Most style guides—MLA, APA, and Chicago, for example—will provide you with instructions for citing images. Organizations may have their own style conventions. Use the conventions for documenting graphics prescribed by your situation. (Chapter 7 will provide you with more detailed help for documenting your sources for text and graphics.)

The rest of this chapter identifies common objects that technical writers use to illustrate their work and suggests when these objects are best used.

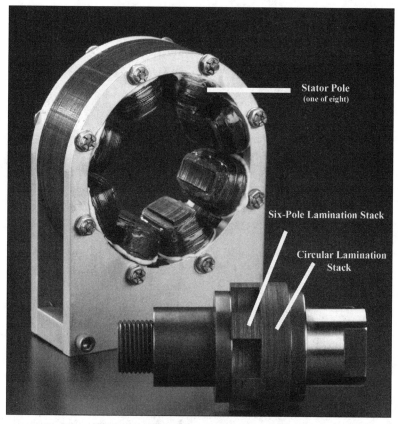

FIGURE 6.1   Photograph of Mechanism. This photograph illustrates the compact design of the Morrison Motor, including its eight stator poles, six-pole lamination stack, and circular lamination stack. The annotations on the photograph point to these specific features.

Source: "Innovative Technologies," *Technology Innovation.* Available online: http://nctn.hq.nasa. gov/innovation/innovation115/B-feature-randd_awards.html (Accessed March 23, 2009.)

Photographs

Photographs have the advantage of realism. As part of a mechanism description, photographs help readers see the mechanism as it really is. Figure 6.1 (*facing page*) shows how words and an annotated photo work together for better understanding. As illustrated in this figure, annotations are typically written horizontally for ease of reading.

Figure 6.2 shows the size of the satellite in comparison to more familiar objects like people and trucks. Such things as coins and actual rulers included in photographs can also efficiently show scale.

FIGURE 6.2   Photograph Showing Size/Scale of an Object.
This historical photograph from NASA's image archive documents the test inflation of a PAGEOS satellite in a blimp hangar at Weeksville, North Carolina. In the photo, the size or scale of the satellite can be easily compared to the sizes of the maintenance trucks and people around it.

Source: Image #: L-1965-06541. *Great Images from NASA (GRIN).* Available online: http://grin.hq.nasa.gov/ABSTRACTS/GPN-2000-001896.html (Accessed March 25, 2009.)

Detecting and Identifying Termites in a Structure

The threat of insects in or around your home can be alarming, especially when those insects can cause structural damage. It is important to know if insects you find around the house are in fact termites or some other crawling insect.

Subterranean termites are found everywhere in the contiguous United States, making the possibility of termite infestation a widespread structural damage problem. Early detection and treatment of termites can drastically reduce the threat of damage to your home.

Detection
Subterranean termites require moisture and usually remain hidden—they may never be seen by the homeowner. Termites often consume the interior portion of a piece of wood but leave the outer shell intact to protect themselves against desiccation (drying out). Therefore, it is easy to overlook the occurrence of termites and mistake a termite-damaged board for sound wood.

One clear indication of termite infestation is the appearance of shelter tubes made of soil and sand and stemming from an underground location near the building. These tubes protect the termites from desiccation as they travel between the soil and your house. Shelter tubes are found commonly in basements of infected homes or running from the soil to the house.

Termites are social insects and live in large colonies with organized caste systems. Worker termites—the most common caste encountered—are likely to be visible during a home inspection. Soldier termites, although far less numerous, are also likely to be found.

Identification
Both worker and soldier termites are white in color, with a small amount of brown on their backs, and are ¼-inch long. Worker termites lack the enlarged, dark yellow head and black mandibles of the soldier termite. Termites of the reproductive caste, called alate, are most commonly confused with ants because of their black color and the presence of wings. The wings of an alate are shed after mating, so wingless reproductive termites closely resemble ants. Fortunately, reproductive alates only fly for a short period in late spring.

Worker   **Soldier**   **Alate**

Four main characteristics differentiate termites from ants:

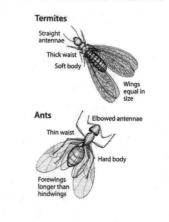

FIGURE 6.3   Photographs with Accompanying Text and Illustrations. The three termite photographs at the top of the page differentiate types while the illustrations underneath explain how to distinguish termites from ants. The accompanying texts contextualize both the photographs and illustrations.

Source: Forest Products Laboratory, Technology Marketing Unit. "Detecting and Identifying Termites in a Structure." *TechLine* (Madison, WI: USDA, U.S. Forest Service, 2006). Available online: http://www.fpl.fs.fed.us/documents/techline/detecting-&-identifying-termites.pdf (Accessed March 20, 2009.)

The photographs in Figure 6.3 (facing page) differentiate termite castes. The accompanying text and diagrams help readers to distinguish termites from ants. Unless they are carefully made, photographs have the disadvantage of including extraneous detail. The strawberry in Figure 6.4 has been carefully photographed so that extraneous detail has been held to a minimum, and adequate emphasis is placed on the fungus.

FIGURE 6.4   Photograph That Minimizes Background Detail. This photograph depicts fungus growth on a strawberry. In it, careful photography minimizes background detail and emphasizes important aspects of fungus growth and location.

Source: Bauer, Scott, *Image Gallery, Image Number K9497-1.* (Washington, D.C.: U.S. Agricultural Research Service, 2006). Available online: http://www.ars.usda.gov/is/graphics/ photos/sep01/k9497-1.htm (Accessed March 17, 2009.)

Drawings

Drawings give you the advantage of control. You can eliminate extraneous detail and easily emphasize whatever you want to emphasize. You can do cutaways of objects that would be difficult or impossible to show in a photograph. Drawings also can be easily annotated. All these advantages are apparent in Figures 6.5 and 6.6 (facing page).

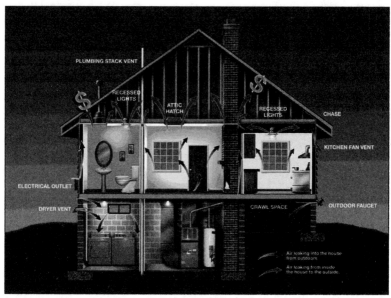

FIGURE 6.5   Drawing with Callouts and Featured Details.
This drawing uses directional arrows and labels to illustrate how energy can drain into and out of a leaky house. Specific sites where energy leaks are labeled, and arrows point to the directional flow of the energy leakage.

Source: Air Sealing and Insulation That Works: Energy Star (Washington, D.C.: U.S. Environmental Protection Agency, 2009). Available online: http://www.energystar.gov/index.cfm?c=behind_the_walls.btw_airsealing (Accessed March 17, 2009.)

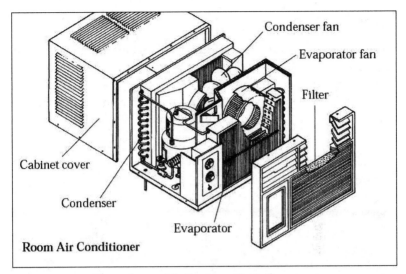

Condenser fan

Evaporator fan

Filter

Cabinet cover

Condenser

Evaporator

Room Air Conditioner

FIGURE 6.6 Drawing with System Details. This diagram uses the cutaway technique to allow viewers to see inside the air conditioner and recognize labeled parts.

Source: "Room Air Conditioners." *A Consumer's Guide to Energy Efficiency and Renewable Energy.* (Washington: U.S. Department of Energy, 2008). Available online: http://apps1.eere.energy.gov/consumer/your_home/space_heating_cooling/index.cfm/ mytopic=12420 (Accessed March 30, 2009.)

Showing Processes

Describing processes is a major activity in technical writing (see pp. 123–125). Many process descriptions benefit from the illustrative power of accompanying graphics. Figure 6.7 shows how a combination of words and illustrations work together to explain to a reader how a process occurs, the replication of the flu virus.

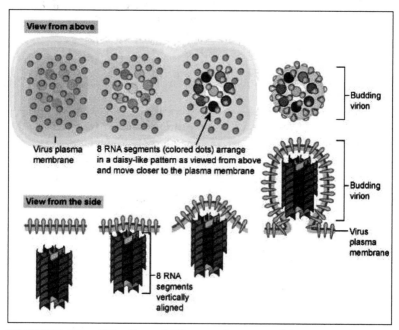

FIGURE 6.7   Words and Illustrations Working Together to Show Process. This illustration uses words and images together to show how genes arrange systematically during flu virus replication.

Source: Townsend, K., "Mystery Solved: How the Flu Virus Makes More of Itself," (Washington, D.C.: National Institute of Allergy and Infectious Diseases (NIAID), 2006). Available online: http://www3.niaid.nih.gov/topics/Flu/Research/basic/MysterySolvedIllustration.htm (Accessed March 25, 2009.)

Figures 6.8 (*below*) and 6.9 (p. 72) illustrate *flowcharts*—graphics that are specifically designed to illustrate decision points or processes. Flowcharts are suitable for all levels of readers.

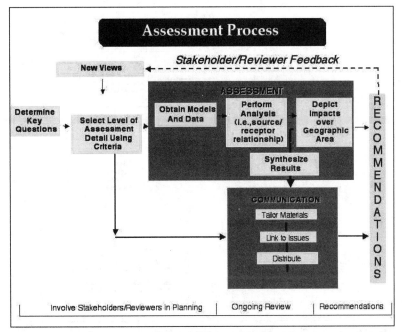

FIGURE 6.8   Flowchart Showing Decision Points. This horizontal flowchart maps an ecological assessment process. Decision points are indicated with text within shaded objects while feedback loops are indicated with arrows.

Source: Clean Air Markets Division, Office of Atmospheric Programs. *How to Measure the Effects of Acid Deposition: A Framework for Ecological Assessments,* (Washington, D.C.: Environmental Protection Agency, 2001). Available online: http://www.epa.gov/ airmarkets/resource/docs/ecoassess.pdf (Accessed March 20, 2009.)

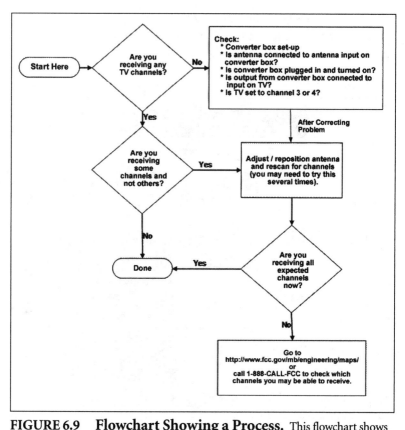

FIGURE 6.9   Flowchart Showing a Process. This flowchart shows how to connect an antenna to a digital television. Answers to the questions in each step lead users in different directions, depending on the outcome of the step.

Source: Consumer and Government Affairs Bureau. "FCC Consumer Facts: Antennas and Digital Television." (Washington: Federal Communications Commission, 2009). Available online: http://www.fcc.gov/cgb/consumerfacts/dtvantennas.html (Accessed March 23, 2009.)

Showing Data

Tables and graphs of all sorts are great word and space savers in display-ing data. With tables and graphs, you can summarize data and show trends and relationships among them.

Tables

Informal tables work well for simple data displays (see pp. 59–60). But for larger and more complex displays, use formal tables. Figure 6.10 illustrates a formal table. Its accompanying annotations describe the table's main features.

Table title with caption → Column heads and subheads → Stub heading → Notes (annotations)

End use[1]	Description	Relative importance, November 2006[2]	Percent change, 12 months ended in December—										
			1997	1998	1999	2000	2001	2002	2003	2004	2005	2006	2007
	Imports												
	All commodities	100.000	-5.2	-6.4	7.0	3.2	-9.1	4.2	2.4	6.7	8.0	2.5	10.6
	All imports, excluding petroleum	82.778	-2.8	-3.3	.0	1.3	-4.5	.3	1.2	3.7	2.4	1.9	3.0
	All imports, excluding fuel	80.324	–	–	–	–	–	.0	1.0	3.0	1.1	2.9	3.1
0	Foods, feeds, and beverages	4.488	1.3	-3.1	-.3	-4.0	-4.7	5.9	3.0	8.0	5.4	4.3	9.6
1	Industrial supplies and materials	35.271	-10.4	-17.1	33.7	13.8	-24.6	21.9	9.5	22.0	25.5	5.0	26.8
	Industrial supplies and materials, excluding petroleum	18.050	-1.7	-6.7	5.1	11.2	-14.6	5.8	7.2	16.4	11.3	4.6	6.7
	Industrial supplies and materials, excluding fuels	15.596	–	–	–	–	–	3.6	6.3	13.4	4.4	11.1	7.4
10	Fuels and lubricants	19.675	-23.8	-36.5	114.7	27.1	-41.9	53.7	13.2	31.5	43.5	.9	42.1
100	Petroleum and petroleum products	17.221	-25.5	-40.8	137.2	17.6	-39.5	56.9	12.8	30.3	42.4	5.3	48.1
2	Capital goods	21.560	-7.4	-5.0	-3.3	-2.1	-2.7	-2.4	-1.1	-.8	-1.3	.5	.8
	Capital goods, excluding computers, peripherals, and semiconductors	15.091	-4.7	-2.1	-1.8	-1.1	-1.0	-1.3	1.2	2.0	1.2	2.3	3.3
3	Automotive vehicles, parts, and engines	14.691	.5	.0	.7	.7	-.2	.5	.9	1.8	.4	.7	2.4
4	Consumer goods, excluding automotives	23.989	-.9	-1.3	-.4	-1.2	-.8	-.7	.1	.9	.6	1.4	1.6
	Exports												
	All commodities	100.000	-1.2	-3.4	.5	1.1	-2.5	1.0	2.2	4.0	2.8	4.5	6.0
	Agricultural commodities	8.115	-2.9	-9.3	-6.8	3.1	-1.8	8.0	13.4	-5.9	4.9	13.5	23.3
	Nonagricultural commodities	91.885	-1.0	-2.7	1.2	.9	-2.5	.4	1.3	5.0	2.6	3.7	4.5
0	Foods, feeds, and beverages	7.350	-3.3	-8.3	-5.7	1.7	-.5	7.9	12.6	-4.5	4.3	13.8	23.4
1	Industrial supplies and materials	30.132	-1.4	-7.1	5.3	3.6	-8.6	5.0	6.8	15.1	8.4	9.0	10.5
	Nonagricultural industrial supplies and materials	28.638	-1.3	-6.9	6.3	3.3	-8.4	4.8	6.3	16.6	8.5	9.2	10.2
2	Capital goods	39.585	-1.6	-1.8	-1.1	.3	-.8	-1.3	-.6	.7	-.5	1.1	1.8
	Capital goods, excluding computers, peripherals, and semiconductors	30.193	-.3	-.7	-.4	.8	.0	.5	.9	2.1	2.1	3.0	3.3
3	Automotive vehicles, parts, and engines	10.683	.8	.5	1.0	.5	.4	.8	.5	1.1	1.0	1.5	1.1
4	Consumer goods, excluding automotives	12.250	.8	-.8	.6	-.4	.2	-.6	.6	1.3	.7	2.1	3.2

Table 1. Annual percent changes in U.S. import and export price indexes for selected categories of goods, 1997–2007

Source: Bureau of Economic Analysis.
Note: Dash indicates data not available.

[1] Category defined by Bureau of Economic Analysis.
[2] Relative importance figures are based on 2005 trade values.

FIGURE 6.10   Complex Table. Annotations label the key parts of the table and describe their functions.

Source: Casey, W. H., and Myron D. Murray, "Import and export price trends, 2007." *Monthly Labor Review.* (Washington: Bureau of Labor Statistics, U.S. Department of Labor, February 2009.) Available online: http://www.bls.gov/opub/mlr/2009/02/art2full.pdf (Accessed March 30, 2009.)

The table in Figure 6.10 is complex enough that its lines serve the useful purpose of separating the data for easy reading. In less complex tables, many of the lines are eliminated (as in Figure 6.11), and white space serves to separate the data. Let ease of reading the table be your guide, but eliminate as much clutter as possible.

When need be, you can interpret your data in headnotes, captions, and annotations. Many of the figures in this chapter illustrate how this

TABLE 9. Differences in Saturated Fat and Calorie Content of Commonly Consumed Foods

This table shows a few practical examples of the differences in the saturated fat content of different forms of commonly consumed foods. Comparisons are made between foods in the same food group (e.g., regular cheddar cheese and low-fat cheddar cheese), illustrating that lower saturated fat choices can be made within the same food group.

Food Category	Portion	Saturated Fat Content (grams)	Calories
Cheese			
• Regular cheddar cheese	1 oz	6.0	114
• Low-fat cheddar cheese	1 oz	1.2	49
Ground beef			
• Regular ground beef (25% fat)	3 oz (cooked)	6.1	236
• Extra lean ground beef (5% fat)	3 oz (cooked)	2.6	148
Milk			
• Whole milk (3.24%)	1 cup	4.6	146
• Low-fat (1%) milk	1 cup	1.5	102
Breads			
• Croissant (med)	1 medium	6.6	231
• Bagel, oat bran (4")	1 medium	0.2	227
Frozen desserts			
• Regular ice cream	½ cup	4.9	145
• Frozen yogurt, low-fat	½ cup	2.0	110
Table spreads			
• Butter	1 tsp	2.4	34
• Soft margarine with zero *trans*	1 tsp	0.7	25
Chicken			
• Fried chicken (leg with skin)	3 oz (cooked)	3.3	212
• Roasted chicken (breast no skin)	3 oz (cooked)	0.9	140
Fish			
• Fried fish	3 oz	2.8	195
• Baked fish	3 oz	1.5	129

Source: ARS Nutrient Database for Standard Reference, Release 17.

FIGURE 6.11   Simple Table

Source: U.S. Department of Agriculture, *Dietary Guidelines for Americans 2005* (Washington, D.C.: U.S. Department of Health and Human Services, 2005). Available online: http://www.health.gov/dietaryguidelines/dga2005/document/pdf/DGA2005.pdf (Accessed March 17, 2009.)

is done. Often, you will interpret your data in the text accompanying your figures. Figure 6.12 illustrates this table-text relationship.

In all the sample tables, notice that whole numbers are lined up on the last digits and fractional numbers on the decimals.

1.1 Race/Ethnicity: Demographic Shifts

Over the 32-year period from 1972 to 2004, there was increasing racial/ethnic diversity among high school seniors (table 1).[2] In 1972, eighty-six percent of high school seniors were White. By 2004, sixty-two percent were White. The percentage of Hispanics in the senior class population increased from 4 percent in 1972 to 15 percent in 2004, and the percentage of Blacks increased from 9 percent to 12 percent between 1972 and 1980.

Table 1.   Percentage of high school seniors, by sex and race/ethnicity: 1972, 1980, 1992, and 2004

Characteristics	Year			
	1972	1980	1992	2004
Sex				
Male	49.9	48.1	50.4	49.9
Female	50.1	51.9	49.6	50.1
Race/ethnicity[1]				
Asian	0.9	1.3	4.5	4.5
Black	8.7	11.6	11.9	13.3
Hispanic	3.5	6.3	10.0	15.0
White	85.8	79.9	72.7	62.3
More than one race	—	—	—	3.9

— Not available.

[1] Due to small sample sizes for the group, the category "American Indian or Alaska Native" was omitted from the tables in this report but included for the purposes of computing percentages.

NOTE: Detail may not sum to totals because of rounding. Asian includes Native Hawaiian or Other Pacific Islander, Black includes African American, and Hispanic includes Latino. All race categories exclude Hispanic or Latino origin.

SOURCE: U.S. Department of Education, National Center for Education Statistics, National Longitudinal Study of the High School Class of 1972 (NLS:72), "Base Year"; High School and Beyond Longitudinal Study of 1980 Seniors (HS&B-Sr:80/86); National Education Longitudinal Study of 1988 (NELS:88/92), "Second Follow-up, Student Survey, 1992"; Education Longitudinal Study of 2002 (ELS:2002/2004), "First Follow-up, 2004."

FIGURE 6.12   Table with Accompanying Text. Tables display data well, but often, they must be explained and interpreted with accompanying text. This example illustrates how to incorporate tables with explanatory text. Note the explanatory text before the table as well as the notes included after the table.

Source: Engels, S., Dalton, B.W., & LoGerfo, L., *Trends Among High School Seniors 1972–2004.* (Washington, National Center for Education Statistics, 2008). Available online: http://nces.ed.gov/pubs2008/2008320.pdf (Accessed March 25, 2009.)

Graphs

Bar, pie, line, and map graphs (pp. 76–79) are all commonly used in technical writing. Figures 6.13 through 6.17 illustrate various kinds of graphs. Each figure caption points out the graph's features and principles of its use. Pictographs or pictograms (p. 80) are sometimes used but mainly for nontechnical audiences. All graphs can be used to summarize and to show trends and relationships. Bar and pie graphs show the relationships among data well. They are good for all audience levels, technical and nontechnical.

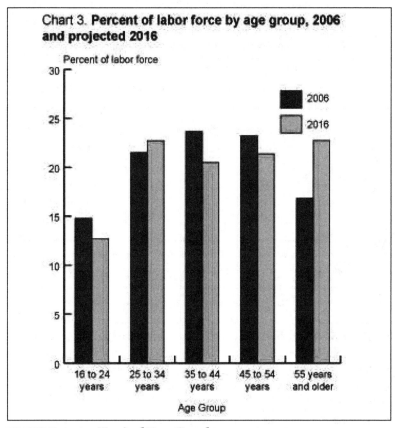

FIGURE 6.13 Typical Bar Graph. When color is not used, use different degrees of shading to distinguish among bars. Cross-hatching is not a good choice because the moiré effect it produces can distract the reader. Avoid clutter of any kind. Do not use a complete grid unless reading the graph precisely is the reason for the graph. Notice that because the highest bar is in the 25% range, the graph only goes to 30%. Do not waste space in graphs.

Source: : Office of Occupational Statistics and Employment Projections, "Tomorrow's Jobs." *Occupational Outlook Handbook.* (Washington: U.S. Bureau of Labor Statistics, 2008–2009). Available online: http://www.bls.gov/oco/oco2003.htm (Accessed March 20, 2009.)

Line graphs are superior to bar graphs in showing the shapes of data. Are the numbers increasing? decreasing? forming a bell curve? Line graphs show these trends well, but be mindful of your audience. Line graphs work well for technical audiences, but unless the graphs are simple, nontechnical audiences may have trouble reading them. Consider using map graphs when there is a geographical component to your data. As you do with tables, provide whatever interpretation is needed on the graph or in the accompanying text.

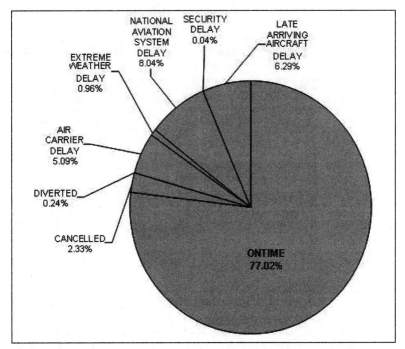

FIGURE 6.14   Pie Graph. This pie chart depicts overall causes for air travel delays in January 2009. In constructing a pie graph, use a rational order for the slices, generally large to small or small to large. Writers occasionally must choose between logical order of slices and horizontal labeling, as is the case in this example. In this pie chart, the author reordered the slices to allow for adequate labeling space. Keep labels horizontal to the page. When there is room, you may label inside the slice, but keep the lettering horizontal.

Source: Aviation Consumer Protection Division, *Air Travel Consumer Report.* (Washington, D.C.: Office of Aviation Enforcement and Proceedings, 2009). Available online: http://airconsumer.ost.dot.gov/reports/2009/March/200903ATCR.PDF (Accessed March 17, 2009.)

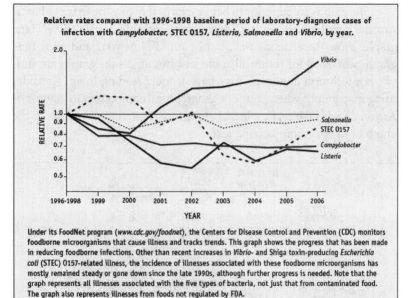

Relative rates compared with 1996-1998 baseline period of laboratory-diagnosed cases of infection with *Campylobacter,* STEC O157, *Listeria, Salmonella* and *Vibrio,* by year.

Under its FoodNet program (*www.cdc.gov/foodnet*), the Centers for Disease Control and Prevention (CDC) monitors foodborne microorganisms that cause illness and tracks trends. This graph shows the progress that has been made in reducing foodborne infections. Other than recent increases in *Vibrio-* and Shiga toxin-producing *Escherichia coli* (STEC) O157-related illness, the incidence of illnesses associated with these foodborne microorganisms has mostly remained steady or gone down since the late 1990s, although further progress is needed. Note that the graph represents all illnesses associated with the five types of bacteria, not just that from contaminated food. The graph also represents illnesses from foods not regulated by FDA.

Source: Centers for Disease Control and Prevention

FIGURE 6.15 **Typical Line Graph.** The lines on this graph are labeled directly on the graph, using lettering horizontal to the page rather than using a key. Lines are kept distinct by using a mixture of dots, dashes, and shadings.

Source: U.S. Drug and Food Administration, *Food Protection Plan: An Integrated Strategy for Protecting the Nation's Food Supply.* (Washington, D.C.: Department of Health and Human Services, 2007). Available online: http://www.fda.gov/oc/initiatives/advance/food/plan.pdf (Accessed March 17, 2009.)

Principles of Tables and Graphs

Graphs and tables should be:

- Clear, uncluttered, and efficient
- Suited to their readers
- Interpreted as needed with notes, captions, annotations, lines, keys, arrows, and text (footnotes are internal to tables and graphs and marked by numbers, letters, or symbols, such as asterisks [*])
- Placed near their text references

- Referred to when needed

- Numbered and have succinct titles: "Average Annual Pay, by State: 2008 and 2009" not "A Summary of Average Annual Pay, by State: 2008 and 2009"

- Well made and aesthetically pleasing but not artsy (too much decoration gets in the way of the message)

- Legible

- Truthful (see pp. 93–97)

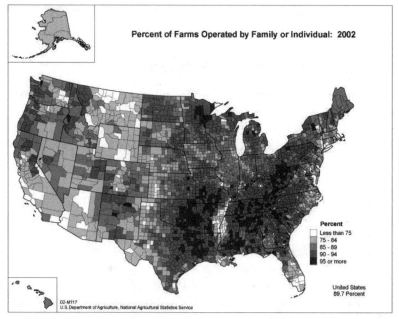

FIGURE 6.16   Map Graph. Map graphs are very effective when geography is a factor, as it is in this graph that depicts the percentage of farms owned by individuals or families, according to the 2002 census report. Different degrees of shading, not cross-hatching, distinguish the different percentages of ownership.

Source: National Agricultural Statistics Service, *The Census of Agriculture 2002: Ag Atlas Maps.* (Washington, D.C.: U.S. Department of Agriculture, 2004). Available online: http://www.agcensus.usda.gov/Publications/2002/Ag_Atlas_Maps/Farms/pdf/02-M117-RGBChor-largetext.pdf (Accessed March 17, 2009.)

Skull and Crossbones | Exclamation Mark | Corrosion | Environment | Flame

FIGURE 6.17   Pictograms. Pictograms are symbols used to convey information to international nontechnical audiences. The pictograms in this example are used in hazard communication, but pictograms are also used to convey accessibility, transportation, and safety messages.

Source: "Pictograms and their Benefits," *Pesticides: International Activities,* (Washington: Environmental Protection Agency, 2008). Available online: http://www. epa.gov/oppfead1/ international/ghs/pictograms.htm (Accessed March 30, 2009.)

Considering Cultural Differences

This chapter has offered you a variety of objects to use when illustrating your ideas. Remember that the objects you choose must match your audience's needs. This is particularly true when you are writing for a global audience. Images can have very different cultural meanings. Colors, for example, have very different meanings across cultures. Green might be used to designate an environmentally friendly option in the United States, whereas in some Asian cultures, it represents sickness. Similarly, an image of a hand giving a thumbs-up would mean everything is okay in the United States and England, but the same image anywhere else would likely insult those readers, for whom the gesture has sexual connotations. These are two simple examples of serious mistakes you can make when your audience is global. The best way to insure that your images send the message you want them to send is to learn as much as possible about cultural differences and always ask a trusted reader who understands cultural differences to review your document before you publish it.

ACTIVITIES

1. Internet documents often use more visuals than print documents. Use an Internet search engine to find a Web site that specializes in instructions. You might look for a Web site that specializes in do-it-yourself home projects or one that teaches its readers how to use a specific piece of software. When you find an instructional Web site, make a list of all the graphics you find in one of the articles housed there. Does the article use pictures, illustrations, videos, or a combination of visuals? Why do you think instructional Web sites use so many different kinds of visuals? Are these visuals effective? Why or why not?

2. With your classmates, make a list of large, international corporations that have a strong Web presence. For example, you might identify automobile, electronic, or furniture manufacturers that produce and sell their products globally. After you have the list, go to one or two of these corporations' Web sites. Do the corporations have multiple sites for different cultures and speakers of different languages? When you find a corporation with multiple sites, compare the visuals on at least two of the sites. Do the Web sites have the same visuals, or are they different? If they are different, how so? What role do you think cultural differences played when the designers were choosing visuals for the Web sites?

CHAPTER ASSIGNMENTS

Assignment 1 for Individual Writers: The Analytical Report

Your report is almost ready to submit to your supervisor. You have focused your message on a specific audience, and you have researched and organized content to meet your audience's needs. In your most recent draft, you added page design to help your reader find the information he or she needs. Now you should consider whether graphics will help deliver your message. What images might you add to improve your report? Are images available that you could copy and insert in your report? Review your report to see where visuals might improve it. Find or create images to use in the report, if you decide they are relevant. Be sure to caption your figures appropriately.

Assignment 2 for a Writing Team: The Recommendation Report

Your recommendation report is near completion. Now your team needs to decide whether visuals would help your readers access the information you are providing. Since this report compares and contrasts multiple products, you might consider what kinds of visuals would allow readers to review features or costs easily. Review the visuals described in this chapter, and select at least one or two kinds of visual to add to your report. Work with your team to create or find the images you want to insert. Be sure to caption your figures appropriately.

7

Write Ethically

Ethical systems, whether religious or philosophical, agree that it is unethical to lie, cheat, and steal. Some systems grant a few exceptions, such as white social lies, a mother stealing for her starving child, and deceiving the enemy in time of war. But in general, the agreement is universal.

Morality consists of being ethical when it would be safer, more convenient, and more profitable to be unethical. Thus, morality does not always come easily. People are often tempted to commit unethical acts for personal gain, out of loyalty to organizations, or out of fear of the consequences they will face if seen as being disloyal—a "whistle blower," for example.

Technical writing has consequences. On the basis of feasibility studies and proposals, governments and businesses spend millions, even billions, of dollars. People follow instructions, expecting that their safety or the safety of their equipment will not be compromised by misstatements. Scientists base future research on past research reports. Researchers who misrepresent results or tell outright lies in their reports can mislead other scientists for years. Therefore, a moral imperative exists for technical and scientific writers to write ethically.

The principles that follow tell you how to prepare technical writing ethically, but they cannot make you act morally. Only you can do that.[1]

Don't Hide or Suppress Unfavorable Data

Imagine that you are an engineer working as an inspector for a state environmental protection agency. You have just inspected the waste disposal facilities of a small city. You find that the city's effluent discharge into a nearby river does not meet state standards. You inform the city engineer, an old college buddy, of the situation. He informs you that the city is aware of the problem and is moving rapidly to solve it. He asks that you keep the effluent problem out of your report. Having the state come down on the city will just delay things, he says.

Should you suppress the information to honor an old friendship? The answer, according to the Engineering Ethics Board, is that you should not.[2] The board has decided in many similar cases that such behavior is unethical. Because public safety is paramount as part of an engineer's ethical code, it overrides not only friendship but even confidentiality agreements.

Similar situations may arise in writing proposals and research reports (see pp. 136–139 and 141–143). In a proposal, the temptation is to hide material that would indicate your company is not suited for the work it proposes to do. In a research report, the data might show that your theory is not as sound as you think. In both situations, the temptation is to hide or suppress the data.

Obviously, the people who read your reports, whatever kinds of reports they may be, put their implicit trust in your preparing honest, complete reports. To violate that trust would be to act immorally.

Don't Exaggerate Favorable Data

Exaggerating favorable data is the reverse of suppressing unfavorable data. In writing a proposal, you might exaggerate the experience of your company's scientists, making them sound more expert than they really are. In a feasibility report or the analysis section of a research report, to support the decision or conclusion you want, you might give favorable data more weight than they deserve.

Is any such exaggeration ever ethical? Where proposals and other sales documents are concerned, the expression "Put your best foot forward" applies. That is, it is legitimate in advertisements and proposals to show how your product or service meets the needs of potential customers. You may do so by emphasizing the strong points of your product or service. You are *expected* to do so by both your organization and your customer. But to be ethical, such emphasis must not distort the facts. For example, in a proposal, you could legitimately emphasize the

PhD in chemical engineering held by your lead investigator, but it would be unethical to imply that her experience matches the needs of the client if, in fact, it does not.

In nonsales documents, such as research reports and feasibility reports, anything less than the relevant data, accompanied by an objective analysis, would be unethical.

Don't Make False Implications

In making a *false implication,* you are actually telling the truth but in a way that leads readers to the wrong conclusion. For example, imagine that you are writing a proposal for construction work in which safety on the job is of major importance. For eight years, your company had an enviable safety record, with an accident rate far below the industry average. However, in the last two years, because the company has not upgraded the equipment used by your employees, the accident rate has soared above the industry average. Even so, the average rate for the past ten years is still slightly below the industry average.

Given this, you could truthfully make the statement "Our average accident rate over the last ten years has been below the industry average." But in doing so, you would be falsely implying that your present operations are being conducted safely. You would be making an unethical statement. Were you to say "Our average accident rate over the last ten years has been *substantially* below the industry average," you would be adding the offense of exaggerating favorable data. Benjamin Franklin had it right when he said, in *Poor Richard's Almanack,* "Half the truth is often a great lie."

Don't Plagiarize

To *plagiarize* is to take the words or ideas of others and present them as your own. Much technical writing is based on research into other people's writing. It is legitimate to use other people's data and ideas, but you must give appropriate credit, as discussed in the next section. It is not legitimate to present the words and sentences of others as your own. You must quote, paraphrase, or summarize.

Just as taking others' words and ideas is stealing, so is taking others' images without their permission. As Chapter 6 discussed, you must seek permission for copyrighted images and apply fair use standards correctly. Even when you have permission, you should credit your sources for the visual resources to take from them as you do for the textual resources.

Seeming exceptions to this principle sometimes occur in technical writing. For example, organizations that write many proposals have large blocks of material available for use by proposal writers, such as descriptions of company facilities and equipment. Because this material, often known as "boilerplate," belongs to the organization and not the original writers, it can be used legitimately without attribution.

Credit Your Sources

Most technical reports require *documentation:* the use of references to identify material you relied on in preparing the report. References credit your sources and allow your readers to find them, if they wish. Many documentation systems exist. If you are preparing an article for a journal, you need to obtain the style book used by that journal as a guide to its documentation system. Likewise, companies, government agencies, university departments, and so forth may all require some special systems of documentation.

It all seems a bit bewildering, but most documentation systems require the same information: author's name, editor's name (if any), title of book or article, and publication data. Publication data in the case of a book include the publisher's name, city of publication, and date of publication. When necessary, publication data may also include information such as edition numbers, volume numbers, and series numbers. Publication data for an article would include the page numbers of the article and the name, volume, number, and date of the periodical.

The differences in documentation systems mainly involve differences in punctuation, capitalization, and the order in which information is presented. The best way to learn a system is to obtain the style book involved and, when you are documenting your report, imitate the appropriate formats down to the last period. Meanwhile, pay attention to what you are seeing and doing, particularly to punctuation, capitalization, and order.

Provided here are samples based on *The Chicago Manual of Style's* author-date system. It is used in many of the natural and physical sciences and in some of the social sciences. It is, therefore, a common system. It is also, as documentation systems go, a fairly simple one.[3] You will find here enough samples to see you through a typical report. If you need more than is provided, see *The Chicago Manual* itself, readily available in most libraries.

Documentation using the author-date system requires adding author-date citations in the text that refer the reader to an alphabetized list called *References* or *Works Cited*. Place each author-date citation within parentheses in the text, as illustrated in Figure 7.1. The actual format depends on the information you have to provide, as illustrated here. As you use these samples, carefully note punctuation, capitalization, and order:

Basic Format

(Baker 1998)

Reference to Specific Page or Division

(Baker 1998, 74)

(Baker 1998, ch. 9)

Reference to Volume

(Cornwall 1999, vol. 2)

Photoperiod regulation may also have other notable consequences. In several conifers, early flushing after short-day (SD) treatment has been reported (for example, Bigras and D'Aoust 1993; Dormling 1968). According to Grossnickle (1991), SD treatment also increased the root growth capacity of western hemlock seedlings at low root temperature.

FIGURE 7.1 Author-Date References Within Text

Source: Adapted from Jaana Luoranen and Risto Rikala, "Growth Regulation and Cold Hardening of Silver Birch Seedlings with Short-Day Treatment," *Tree Planters' Notes* 48 (1997): 65.

Reference to Volume and Page

(Cornwall 1999, 2:67)

Two or Three Authors

(Fielding and Meaders 1996)

(Manchester, Kehoe, and Holl 1998)

More Than Three Authors

(Osborn et al. 1993)

Author with Two or More Works of Same Date Cited

(Larsen, 1998a)

(Larsen, 1998b)

Organization as Author

(Landings Corporation 1996)

Multiple References in Same Parentheses

(Baker 1998; Lewis 1993; Noelani 1995)

Author's Name Used in Text

(2000)

(2000, 74)

Note: When you cite authors directly in text, do not repeat their names in parenthetical citations (see Figure 7.1).

Figure 7.2 illustrates how to construct an alphabetized reference list. Here are examples of typical entries for such a list:

Basic Book

Winchester, S. 1999. *The professor and the madman.* New York: HarperCollins.

Note: This entry lists, in order, the author, date, title, city of publication, and publisher. You may use initials or full names of authors, but be consistent throughout the reference list. The names of publishing companies are usually given in short forms. For example, *HarperCollins Publishers, Inc.* is listed as *HarperCollins*.

Book with Two or More Authors

Spoehr, K. T., and S. W. Lehmkuble. 1982. *Visual information processing*. San Francisco: W. H. Freeman.

Note: Do not use "and others" in a reference list. List all the authors—last name first for the first author, and normal order for the rest.

Book with Editor

Frank, F. W., and P. A. Treichler, eds. 1989. *Language, gender, and professional writing*. New York: MLA.

REFERENCES

Boberg, T. C., *Thermal Methods of Oil Recovery*. (New York: Wiley, 1988).

Davis, E. L., "Steam Injection for Soil and Aquifer Remediation," *EPA: Water Ground Issue,* 1998. http://www.epa.gov/ada/download/issue/steaminj.pdf

Itamura, M. T., and K. S. Udell, "An Analysis of Optimal Cycling Time and Ultimate Chlorinated Hydrocarbon Removal from Heterogeneous Media Using Cyclic Steam Injection," *Proceedings of ASME Heat Transfer and Fluids Engineering Divisions,* HTD-Vol. 321, FED-Vol. 233 (New York: ASME Press, 1995): 57–62.

Keyes, B. R., and G. D. Silcox, "Fundamental Study of the Thermal Desorption of Toulene from Montmorillonite Clay Particles," *Environmental Science Technology* 28 (1994): 840–49.

FIGURE 7.2   Reference List

Note: Use *ed.* for *editor, eds.* for two or more *editors,* and *trans.* for singular or plural *translators.* Names of organizations likely to be known to readers are often abbreviated—in this case, *MLA* for the *Modern Language Association.*

Organization as Author

Department of Agriculture (DOA). 1999. *National forestry manual.* Washington, DC: GPO.

Note: *GPO* is a widely used abbreviation for the *Government Printing Office,* which prints most books published by the federal government.

Later Edition

Fuller, Jane. 1999. *The history of Skidaway Island.* 2nd ed. Savannah, GA: Pilgrim Press.

Note: When the city of publication is not well-known, use additional identification, such as the state abbreviation.

Essay in an Edited Collection

Cooper, M. 1989. The ecology of writing. In *Writing as social action,* ed. M. M. Cooper and M. Holzman, 1–13. Portsmouth, NH: Boynton/Cook Heinemann.

Basic Journal Entry

Cushman, J. 1999. Critical literacy and institutional language. *Research in the Teaching of English* 33:245–74.

Note: This entry lists, in order, the author, date, article, journal, volume, and inclusive page numbers for the article. Use this form for journals that are paginated by volume, rather than issue. Treat the names of multiple authors for articles as you do multiple authors for books. Cite page numbers as in these examples: 1–13; 16–28; 200–206; 201–8; 224–29; 1156–68.

Entry for Journals Paginated by Issue

Hall, L. 1999. Taking charge of menopause. *FDA Consumer* 33, no. 6 (November–December): 17–21.

Note: Use the issue number and the date in the journal masthead—for example, *December, Fall, 18 June,* and so forth. Put *no.* (for *number*) to distinguish the issue number from the volume number.

Entry for Popular Magazine

Boyer, Peter J. 2000. DNA on trial. *New Yorker,* 17 January, 42–53.

Paper Read at a Meeting

Colomb, G. G., and J. Simutis. 1992. Written conversation and the transition to college. Paper presented at the Computers and Writing Conference, Ann Arbor, MI.

Personal Communication

Cunningham, D. 1999. Interview by author. Oklahoma City, OK, October 28.

Note: Identify the nature of the communication: letter, telephone call, e-mail, interview, and so forth.

Two Entries for an Author

Eisner, E. W. 1985. *The educational imagination.* 2nd ed. New York: Macmillan.

———. 1991. *The enlightened eye.* New York: Macmillan.

Note: Use three long dashes (or six hyphens) for another entry by the same author.

Internet Documentation

Given the vast and ever-changing nature of the Internet, citing sources found online can be a challenge. Authors' names may be lacking or abbreviated. Articles may not have titles. Because of revisions, dates of publication may change frequently or be missing altogether. Many Internet sources are not paginated.

Therefore, when you compile Internet citations in your list of references, you will need to use different forms than you use for books and articles. Despite the differences in form, the purposes are the same: to give credit to the original source and to enable the reader to locate the source.

The system shown here is based on *The Chicago Manual*'s citation style. The basic parts of the citations used in this system are as follow, subject to availability and applicability:

- Author's name, last name first (if there is more than one author, put the names of subsequent authors in normal order). If only the author's alias or log-in name is available, use that. If no identifier is available for the author, use the best information you have, such as the name of the document or site.
- Title of document and title of complete work
- Volume, version, or file number
- Last date of document
- Access information
- Date accessed

The following examples illustrate the use of this system for several different kinds of sources (see also Figure 7.2):

World Wide Web (WWW) Site

Geoff Koch and Rachel Carr, "Probing the Heart of the Atom," *Symmetry* 6, no. 1 (March 2009), <http://symmetrymagazine .org/cms/?pid=1000687> (4 May 2009).

File Transfer Protocol (FTP)

Irons, M. and G. Manchester. 10 August 1999. The vault of the Sidney Opera House. ftp://ftp.cchs.su.edu.au/ (5 January 2000).

Listserv

AliceB. 12 December 1999. Re: trigeminal neuralgia. *TN-L Trigeminal & Facial Neuralgia*. tnl@listserv.uark.edu (6 February 2000).

E-mail

Cunningham, D. 1999. E-mail to author, 28 October.

Construct parenthetical author-date citations in your text for Internet sources just as you do for other forms of publication (see pp. 87–88). As with books and articles, the actual format of the parenthetical Internet reference depends on the information you have. For example, the reference in your text for the listserv citation on page 92 would be as follows:

(AliceB 1999)

Construct Ethical Graphs

Like words, graphs can lie, suppress, exaggerate, and tell half-truths. The basic rule for integrity in graphs is that the physical representation of the data must accurately reflect them.[4] For example, if the number of accidents in a plant has increased and decreased only slightly over the years, the curve on the graph representing those changes should be very shallow. However, by drawing a narrow graph, a graphic artist can end up with a steep curve and thus misrepresent the changes. See Figure 7.3 (p. 94) for an example of an unethical bar graph.

Numbers that change in only one direction can be misrepresented by changing the physical dimensions of the graph in two directions. For example, in a bar graph, increasing the sizes of the bars both vertically and horizontally will increase the area of the bars out of proportion to the actual increases in data, thus greatly exaggerating them. Pictographs that portray physical objects, such as people and factories, often lack integrity because they increase in two or three dimensions while the underlying numbers increase in only one (see Figure 7.4, p. 95).

Because of the devaluation of the dollar caused by inflation, graphing in *current* dollars can distort the true growth in prices, wages, and figures such as the federal debt. In dealing with dollars, use *constant* dollars. In constant dollars, the value given for the dollar for a specific year is 1. All dollar values for years before and after the chosen year are then valued in proportion to the constant in a way that reflects inflation. For example, a dollar value for a year before the chosen year may have a value

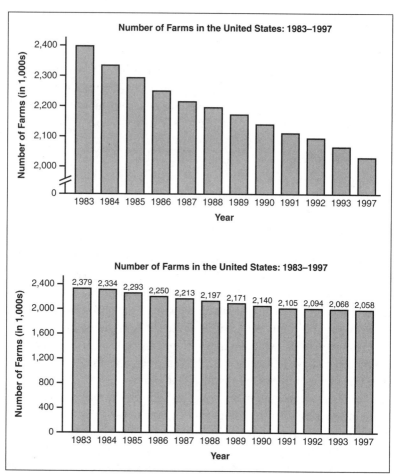

FIGURE 7.3   Vertical Misrepresentation of Data. The *top* graph greatly exaggerates the decline in family farms for the years 1983 to 1997. The *bottom* graph represents the data accurately. Also in the bottom graph, labeling each bar with the appropriate number increases the integrity of the graph.

Source: Data from U.S. Department of Commerce, *Statistical Abstract of the United States,* 118th ed. (Washington, DC: GPO, 1998), 670.

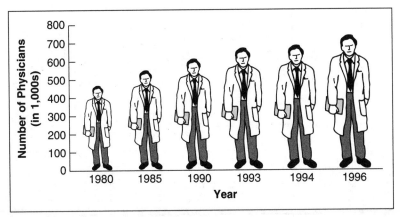

FIGURE 7.4   Inaccurate Pictograph. Because the "physician" figures in this pictograph grow in more than one dimension, they grow disproportionately to the underlying data. A well-constructed bar chart showing the same data would not be as dramatic but would represent the data accurately.

Source: Data from U.S. Department of Commerce, *Statistical Abstract of the United States,* 118th ed. (Washington, DC: GPO, 1998), 129.

of 1.041, and one after may have a value of 0.984. The table in Figure 7.5 (p. 96) shows how this system works. The graph in Figure 7.6 (p. 97) demonstrates the inaccuracy of graphing in current dollars compared to graphing in constant dollars.

Inexperienced graph readers can be easily misled by unethical graphs. Experienced graph readers will spot graphs that misrepresent data and, therefore, mistrust the author of the report. You owe it to yourself and to your readers to graph ethically.

No. 771. Purchasing Power of the Dollar: 1950 to 1997

[Indexes: PPI, 1982 = $1.00; CPI, 1982–84 = $1.00. Producer prices prior to 1961, and consumer prices prior to 1964, exclude Alaska and Hawaii. Producer prices based on finished goods index. Obtained by dividing the average price index for the 1982 = 100, PPI; 1982–84 = 100, CPI base periods (100.0) by the price index for a given period and expressing the result in dollars and cents. Annual figures are based on average monthly data.]

YEAR	ANNUAL AVERAGE AS MEASURED BY—		YEAR	ANNUAL AVERAGE AS MEASURED BY—		YEAR	ANNUAL AVERAGE AS MEASURED BY—	
	Producer prices	Consumer prices		Producer prices	Consumer prices		Producer prices	Consumer prices
1950	$3.546	$4.151	1966	2.841	3.080	1982	1.000	1.035
1951	3.247	3.846	1967	2.809	2.993	1983	0.984	1.003
1952	3.268	3.765	1968	2.732	2.873	1984	0.964	0.961
1953	3.300	3.735	1969	2.632	2.726	1985	0.955	0.928
1954	3.289	3.717	1970	2.545	2.574	1986	0.969	0.913
1955	3.279	3.732	1971	2.469	2.466	1987	0.949	0.880
1956	3.195	3.678	1972	2.392	2.391	1988	0.926	0.846
1957	3.077	3.549	1973	2.193	2.251	1989	0.880	0.807
1958	3.012	3.457	1974	1.901	2.029	1990	0.839	0.766
1959	3.021	3.427	1975	1.718	1.859	1991	0.822	0.734
1960	2.994	3.373	1976	1.645	1.757	1992	0.812	0.713
1961	2.994	3.340	1977	1.546	1.649	1993	0.802	0.692
1962	2.985	3.304	1978	1.433	1.532	1994	0.797	0.675
1963	2.994	3.265	1979	1.289	1.380	1995	0.782	0.656
1964	2.985	3.220	1980	1.136	1.215	1996	0.762	0.638
1965	2.933	3.166	1981	1.041	1.098	1997	0.759	0.623

FIGURE 7.5   Purchasing Power of the Dollar: 1950–1997

Source: U.S. Department of Commerce, *Statistical Abstract of the United States,* 118th ed. (Washington, DC: GPO, 1998), Table 771.

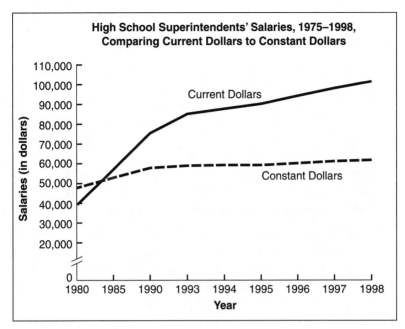

FIGURE 7.6   Comparison of Current Dollars to Constant Dollars. The curve using "Current Dollars" gives the false impression that high school superintendents have more than doubled their buying power over an 18-year period. The curve using "Constant Dollars" accurately shows that the increase was more modest than that.

Source: Data from U.S. Department of Commerce, *Statistical Abstract of the United States,* 118th ed. (Washington, DC: GPO, 1998), 176.

Don't Lie

Many of the previous principles deal with unethically shading the truth. The final principle is all encompassing: *Do not lie.* Scientists and technicians are overwhelmingly honest, but there are exceptions. A scientist has fabricated case histories to support his psychological theories. A few scientists have plagiarized the works of others. These few have been outright liars. Science and technology are built on trust. To violate that trust is to shake the very foundation on which science and technology are built.

ACTIVITIES

1. Many professional organizations have developed their own codes of ethics. Both the Society for Technical Communication (www.stc.org) and the Association of Teachers of Technical Writing (www.attw.org) have specific codes for how members of these organizations should practice. Find the code of ethics for either of these organizations or for an organization that you belong to. Bring the code to class and compare the ethical codes that you and your classmates have found. What are the ethical and unethical behaviors described in these codes? Why are codes important for professions?

2. In the news, we frequently read about individuals who have violated their professional ethics codes. Use the Internet or your campus library to find a story about someone who violated an ethical code. Bring this story to class and discuss what went wrong. How could these ethical violations have been avoided?

CHAPTER ASSIGNMENTS

Assignment 1 for Individual Writers: The Analytical Report

The last element of technical writing to consider before you complete your report is whether you have been ethical in presenting the information in it. Using the guidelines in this chapter, consider whether you have prepared your work ethically. Have you acknowledged all resources you have drawn on? Have you included references if you cited specific resources or borrowed graphics? If not, revise your report to include this missing information.

When you have checked your document, review it carefully one last time to make sure you have successfully met your readers' needs and written the most professional document possible. When you are satisfied that your work is the best it can be, submit your report to your instructor.

Assignment 2 for a Writing Team: The Recommendation Report

Your team has almost finished your recommendation report. The final check is to review for ethical writing. Use the guidelines in this chapter to review your document to make sure you have been truthful, thorough, and unbiased in your recommendation. Have you cited your sources, including visual resources? If necessary, revise your document once more to include any missing information.

When you are sure your report is completely and ethically written, review it one last time with your teammates. If the work is the best it can be, submit it to your instructor.

PART TWO

The Formats of Technical Writing

8

Elements of Reports

This chapter describes every element you *might* need in a report, from the title page to the reference list. How many of these elements you actually use depends on the needs of your audience, the situation in which you are writing, and the type of report you are writing. A large-scale company report might need every one of the elements. A short, informal, intraoffice report might need only a title page, introduction, discussion, and summary.

Chapter 9, Formats of Reports, recommends the elements needed for specific kinds of reports, such as feasibility reports. Before you learn conventions for specific types of reports, however, this chapter introduces you to elements that are typical in many reports. Formal reports often respond to specific writing assignments, such as request for proposals (RFPs). RFPs are specific writing assignments that describe what kinds of information to include in your report and how to organize it. If you do not have a formal writing assignment that designates content and organization or you are writing an informal internal report, then you will need to select elements carefully to be sure you include all the information your audience needs.

If you are in doubt, how do you decide what to include in your report? Use your work plan to remind you of your communication purpose, audience, and situation. A report that has too much or too little information will fail to accomplish its purpose. That is why your work plan is so important. If you have planned well, your message will reach its target.

The rest of this chapter overviews the elements that readers expect in different kinds of reports. The first elements are found more often in formal reports while the latter half, beginning with abstracts and summaries, are typically included in both formal and informal reports.

Title Page

Formal reports, which are most often written for audiences external to your organization, begin with a *title page*. The title page will likely be the first thing a reader examines. It should, therefore, be useful and attractive.

To be useful, the title page should contain, at a minimum, the following information: the title of the report, the name of the author(s), the name of the person(s) for whom the report is written, and the date of the report. If those people writing and receiving the report have titles or organizational affiliations, include them as well. Figure 8.1 (p. 104) shows a basic title page.

In professional situations, the title page may also include items such as contract numbers, security codes, logos, and abstracts. Generally speaking, in such situations, you will be given instructions or samples to work from. If in doubt, ask for help from experienced people in your organization.

The wording of the title is important. Be sure it is complete enough to make your subject clear, but do not add useless words. The title "Volcanic Gases Create Air Pollution on the Island of Hawaii" is good because it makes clear the subject of the report and contains nothing superfluous. A title such as "Gases Create Pollution in Hawaii" would not truly identify the subject and would almost certainly mislead the reader into thinking the subject is broader than it is. On the other hand, adding phrases such as "A Report Concerning" or "A Study of" provides no useful information.

Make your title pages attractive by keeping them uncluttered and well-balanced. Don't let word-processing capabilities or templates tempt you into using a hodgepodge of type styles and excessive ornamentation. The judicious use of some boldface type and, when appropriate, a logo will generally suffice.

Letter of Transmittal

Another element of a formal report is the *letter of transmittal*. Most technical reports go to one person or to a small group of persons. Often, a letter of transmittal is used to formalize the forwarding of the report. When used, the letter of transmittal gives the following basic information: a statement of transmittal, the reason for the report, and the subject and purpose of the report. If you think it is appropriate, you may also point out special features of the report (such as specially prepared charts and graphs) and acknowledge people or organizations who have been helpful in preparing it. See Figure 8.2 (p. 105) for an example of a typical letter of transmittal.

Efficient, Economical Ways of Cleaning Polluted Soils and Ground Water

Prepared for
Professor James Morris
ET 232
Pollution Control Technology

By
Thelma Miller

29 February 2008

FIGURE 8.1   **Basic Title Page**

Weaver Hall
University of California
Santa Cruz, CA 95064
29 February 2008

Professor James Morris
Department of Environmental Technology
University of California
Santa Cruz, CA 95064

Dear Professor Morris:

I submit the accompanying report, "Efficient, Economical Ways of Cleaning Polluted Soils and Ground Water," in accordance with the requirements for ET 232, Pollution Control Technology.

This report describes the cleansing of polluted soils and ground water by two methods: steam injection and high-voltage electricity. In many situations, these methods are more efficient and economical than the pumping methods currently in use.

The report analyzes why corporations are not using these better techniques when they are appropriate and concludes that changes in existing state and federal environmental regulations are needed to bring about their use. Needed changes are recommended.

Sincerely,

Thelma Miller

Thelma Miller

FIGURE 8.2   Letter of Transmittal

In some circumstances, you may point out certain implications of the report and even state your major conclusions and recommendations. How much you include in your letter of transmittal depends to some extent on whether your report includes features such as executive summaries or informative abstracts (features that will be explained shortly). To aid in reader accessibility and selectivity, a certain amount of redundancy is permissible and even desirable in report format, but don't overdo it.

Depending on your organization's policy, the letter of transmittal may be placed immediately before or after the title page. Alternatively, the letter of transmittal may be mailed separately as notice that the report is forthcoming.

Preface

Sometimes, formal reports are intended for large groups of people. For example, environmental impact statements are used to explain the environmental impacts of building large projects, such as highways. Because many people are concerned with such impacts, such reports are widely circulated. When this is the case, a *preface* is more appropriate than a letter of transmittal. A preface differs little from a letter of transmittal except in format (see Figure 8.3).

PREFACE

This report has been prepared for the California Environmental Protection Agency by the Department of Environmental Technology at the University of California at Santa Cruz. It describes the cleansing of polluted soils and ground water by two methods: steam injection and high-voltage electricity. In many situations, these methods are more efficient and cost-effective than the pumping methods currently in use.

The report analyzes why California corporations are not using these better techniques when they are appropriate and concludes that changes in existing California and federal environmental regulations are needed to bring about their use. The report recommends needed changes that are in keeping with the agency's stated mission of protecting public health "in an equitable, efficient, and cost-effective manner."

FIGURE 8.3   Preface

Table of Contents

Long formal reports also include a *table of contents* (TOC). A TOC aids accessibility and selectivity by locating the major divisions and subdivisions within your report for readers. All division and subdivision headings in your TOC must match, word for word, the corresponding headings within the report. You may have more than three levels of headings within your report (see pp. 49–54), but generally, it is not practical for the TOC to have more than three levels. If you make your TOC overcomplicated, it will quickly become as difficult to find things in the TOC as in the report.

In constructing your TOC, use some combination of capital letters, boldface, and indentations to make the different levels of headings distinct from one another. As with the title page, however, do not be tempted into excessive complication by your word-processing capabilities. Figure 8.4 shows a typical TOC, suitable for a student report. You can find many other examples in the books, magazines, and journals that you read.

CONTENTS

List of Illustrations	**iii**
Introduction	**1**
Steam-Enhanced Extraction	**2**
Methodology	3
Cost	5
Successful Use	6
Solvent cleanup	6
Creosote cleanup	7
High-Voltage Electricity	**8**
Methodology	9
Cost	11
Successful Use	12
Gasoline cleanup	12
Diesel oil cleanup	13
Regulatory Problems and Solutions	**14**
Existing California and Federal Regulations	15
Recommended Changes	16

FIGURE 8.4 **Table of Contents**

List of Illustrations

If you have more than three or four figures and tables in your report, you may want to include a listing of them immediately after the TOC (see Figure 8.5). If you mix tables and figures in one list, call it a *List of Illustrations*. If you have separate lists, call them *List of Tables* and *List of Figures*. You can be even more specific. For example, if you have many maps, create a *List of Maps*.

As with report titles, illustration titles should describe the illustrations adequately but not include useless language, such as "A Map Showing. . . ." (See also Chapter 6.)

Glossary

Analyze your audience. Are you using words that are unfamiliar to your readers? If so, you will need to define those words. If you have only a few to define, you may choose to do so in the report—perhaps in the introduction or where you use the word for the first time. If you use many unfamiliar words, say, as many as ten, consider using a *glossary*—that is, a list of definitions (see Figure 8.6). Glossaries typically use parallel sentence

<table>
<tr><td colspan="3" align="center">**LIST OF FIGURES**</td></tr>
<tr><td></td><td></td><td align="right">*Page*</td></tr>
<tr><td>2-1</td><td>Mercury Cell Replacement with Membrane Cells for Chlor-Alkali Production Facilities</td><td align="right">2-9</td></tr>
<tr><td>2-2</td><td>Carbon Filter Bed Design</td><td align="right">2-20</td></tr>
<tr><td>2-3</td><td>Comparison of Mercury Removal Efficiencies with Activated Carbon Injection</td><td align="right">2-31</td></tr>
<tr><td>2-4</td><td>Equilibrium Adsorption Capacity of Elemental Mercury (Hg(0)) and Mercuric Chloride (HgCl$_2$) by a Lignite-Based Activated Carbon</td><td align="right">2-42</td></tr>
<tr><td>4-1</td><td>Example Methodology of a Benefits Analysis</td><td align="right">4-10</td></tr>
<tr><td>B-1</td><td>Spray Cooling System</td><td align="right">B-12</td></tr>
<tr><td>B-2</td><td>Carbon Injection System</td><td align="right">B-12</td></tr>
</table>

FIGURE 8.5   List of Figures

Source: Office of Air Quality Planning and Standards and Office of Research and Development, *An Evaluation of Mercury Control Technology and Costs,* vol. 8 of *Mercury Study Report to Congress* (Washington, DC: U.S. Environmental Protection Agency, 1997), x.

GLOSSARY

Aquifer   An underground geological formation, or group of formations, containing water. Are sources of groundwater for wells and springs.

Attenuation   The process by which a compound is reduced in concentration over time, through absorption, adsorption, degradation, dilution, and/or transformation. an also be the decrease with distance of sight caused by attenuation of light by particulate pollution.

Erosion   The wearing away of land surface by wind or water, intensified by land-clearing practices related to farming, residential or industrial development, road building, or logging.

Ground Water   The supply of fresh water found beneath the Earth's surface, usually in aquifers, which supply wells and springs. Because ground water is a major source of drinking water, there is growing concern over contamination from leaching agricultural or industrial pollutants or leaking underground storage tanks.

Pilot Tests   Testing a cleanup technology under actual site conditions to identify potential problems prior to full-scale implementation.

Potentially Responsible Party (PRP)   Any individual or company—including owners, operators, transporters or generators—potentially responsible for, or contributing to a spill or other contamination at a Superfund site. Whenever possible, through administrative and legal actions, EPA requires PRPs to clean up hazardous sites they have contaminated.

Precipitation   Removal of hazardous solids from liquid waste to permit safe disposal; removal of particles from airborne emissions as in rain (e.g. acid precipitation).

Record of Decision (ROD)   A public document that explains which cleanup alternative(s) will be used at National Priorities List sites where, under CERCLA, Trust Funds pay for the cleanup.

Sedimentation   Letting solids settle out of wastewater by gravity during treatment.

Soil Gas   Gaseous elements and compounds in the small spaces between particles of the earth and soil. Such gases can be moved or driven out under pressure.

Water Table   The level of groundwater.

*It is important in reports to use correct grammar and punctuation as the material will serve as a public source of information.

FIGURE 8.6   Glossary

Source: U.S. Environmental Protection Agency, "Superfund Fact Sheet," (1998), http://www.epa.gov/glossary/ (Accessed June 3, 2009).

fragments as definitions, most often noun phrases. However, if the definitions are extended past the fragments, complete sentences are used, as in the entry for *Ground Water* in Figure 8.6. (Also see Chapter 2 for more about definitions.)

You may locate the glossary in the front of your report, probably after the TOC or the list of illustrations, or in the back as an appendix. Be sure to state in your introduction where the glossary is. Some report writers go so far as to use boldface or a symbol of some sort (such as an asterisk) to identify in the text words that are defined in the glossary.

List of Symbols

Scientific and technical writing often includes a good many symbols, most of which need definition. As with words, you can define symbols in the text of your report or in a separate list (see Figure 8.7). The *list of symbols* is usually located in the front of the report, following the list of illustrations or the glossary.

	LIST OF SYMBOLS AND NOTATIONS
n	Total porosity
n_e	Effective porosity
ppm	Parts per million
TDS	Total dissolved solids
V_c	Velocity of contaminant through a control volume
V_p	Velocity of water through a control volume

FIGURE 8.7   **List of Symbols and Notations**

Abstracts and Summaries

The readers of technical reports are busy people. They often need to have the key points of the reports they read summarized for them (see Chapters 2 and 3). *Abstracts* and *summaries* serve that purpose, and, because they are so useful, abstracts or summaries are typically included in both formal and informal technical reports. Each condenses the most important facts, generalizations, conclusions, and recommendations of a report into a concise statement. Whether you call that statement an *abstract* or a *summary* depends mainly on the kind of report you are writing and where you locate the statement.

Many scientific and technical reports have a summarizing statement near the front. In that position, the statement is most often called an *abstract*. If placed at the end of the report, the statement is usually called a *summary*. Reports written specifically for executives usually contain a special kind of summary called an *executive summary,* most often placed just before the introduction. The sample report formats in Chapter 9 make clear where summaries and abstracts are placed in various kinds of reports.

Figure 8.8 (p. 112) is a summary found at the end of an article written for a mixed audience of generalists and specialists. It concisely restates the key facts and generalizations of the article.

Figure 8.9 (p. 113) is an abstract that appears before a report of scientific research. Like most abstracts, it is meant to stand alone, if need be. Therefore, it contains the key facts, generalizations, and conclusions of the report.

Figure 8.10 (p. 114) is an executive summary. Like many such summaries, its emphasis is on the "bottom line"—that is, the conclusions of the report.

A *descriptive abstract* is different from other abstracts and summaries. As its name implies, it describes the report. That is, rather than summarizing the report, it briefly tells what will be found in the report, thereby prompting readers to decide whether they want to read the report that follows. In a company report, the descriptive report is often placed on the

SUMMARY

Laboratory studies and field demonstrations have demonstrated the ability of steam injection to effectively recover volatile and semivolatile contaminants from the subsurface. However, in order to effectively and efficiently apply this process, it is important to characterize the site adequately to determine the horizontal and vertical distribution of the contaminant, and the preferred flow paths for the injected steam. This information is critical to the design of the steam injection and extraction system. Effective operation of the system will likely include cyclic operation of steam injection and vacuum extraction after steam breakthrough at the extraction well has occurred. Advantages of steam injection over other remediation techniques include the fact that excavation is not required, potential contaminants are not injected to the subsurface, and potentially much more rapid remediations are possible. Without a doubt, the initial capital costs for steam injection are higher than those for a system that relies on removal of soil gases without heating, such as vacuum extraction. However, the accelerated removal rates can lower the total cost of cleanup by reducing the time required for the remediation, thus reducing the overall operating costs (Udell and Stewart, 1989). In addition, the higher temperatures can increase the amount of semivolatile organics that are recovered and the removal efficiencies from clay soils by increasing the volatilization and desorption from soil surfaces. In systems where the volatilization is limited by a low volatility of the contaminant or strong adsorption onto a solid phase, the temperature of the system may actually determine the cleanup level that can be attained. There will undoubtedly be trade offs between the efficiency of the cleanup and the cost of the treatment process.

FIGURE 8.8   Summary

Source: Eva L. Davis, "Steam Injection for Soil and Aquifer Remediation," *EPA: Ground Water Issue* (January 1998): 14, http://www.epa.gov/tio/tsp/download/steaminj.pdf (Accessed June 3, 2009).

title page. In a journal article, it may be placed above or below the article title, serving much like an extended title. What follows is typical:

> This article describes the usefulness of applying the principles of business process re-engineering to online documentation. Further, it presents the benefits of user-centered design, iterative user and task feedback, and an interdisciplinary design team.[1]

ABSTRACT

The document provides comprehensive information on the use of in situ air stripping to remediate contaminated groundwater at the U.S. Department of Energy (DOE) Savannah River site in Aiken, South Carolina. An estimated 3.5 million pounds of solvents were discharged from aluminum forming and metal finishing operations performed at the site between 1958 and 1985, with over 2 million pounds sent to an unlined settling basin. A pump and treat program has been ongoing since 1985 for removal of VOCs from the groundwater and a field demonstration using in situ air stripping was conducted from 1990 to 1993. The demonstration was part of a program at Savannah River to investigate the use of several technologies to enhance the pump and treat system. The in situ air stripping process increased VOC removal over conventional vacuum extraction from 109 pounds per day to 129 pounds per day. This document includes a technology description and performance report, as well as discussions of technology applicability and alternatives, cost, regulatory/policy requirements and issues, lessons learned, and references. Appendices provide more detailed information on demonstration site characteristics, technology descriptions, performance, and commercialization/intellectual property are also included.

FIGURE 8.9   Abstract

Source: "In Situ Air Stripping of Contaminated Groundwater at U.S. Department of Energy, Savannah River Site—Aiken, South Carolina," *Remediation Case Studies: Groundwater Treatment*, http://www.clu-in.org/download/remed/sveresgd.pdf (Accessed June 3, 2009).

EXECUTIVE SUMMARY

The EPA's Robert S. Kerr Environmental Research Laboratory evaluated the following in situ technologies for remediation of dense nonaqueous phase liquids (DNAPLs) contamination occurring below the ground water table: biological, electrolytic, containment and ground modification, soil washing, air stripping, and thermal.

Remediation of DNAPLs faces challenges posed by the site stratigraphy and heterogeneity, the distribution of the contamination and the physical and chemical properties of the DNAPL. A successful technology has to be able to overcome the problems posed by the site complexity and be able to modify the properties of the DNAPL to facilitate recovery, immobilization or degradation. In addition, methodology must be adaptable to different site conditions and must be able to meet the regulatory goals.

Thermally based technologies are regarded as among the most promising, with steam enhanced extraction (SEE) as probably the most promising candidate. The next group of promising technologies are the soil washing technologies because they can manipulate chemical equilibria and reduce capillary forces. A blend of alkalis, cosolvents and surfactants is probably the best combination for a soil washing application, each important for its own reasons. Alkalis can saponify certain DNAPLs and affect wetability and sorption; cosolvents provide viscous stability and enhance solubility and mass transfer between the aqueous phase and the DNAPL; surfactants have the largest impacts on solubility and interfacial tension reduction. Water flooding is best applied in highly contaminated areas as a precursor to these methods.

The thermal and soil washing technologies are considered as best suited for areas that are highly contaminated with DNAPLs. However, these techniques by themselves still may not be able to achieve the currently mandated regulated cleanup standards. Thus, consideration should be given to using these technologies in combination with the technologies suitable for long-term plume management. The bio-remediation techniques and permeable treatment walls hold the best promise.

FIGURE 8.10   Executive Summary

Source: Adapted from William H. Engelmann, "DNAPL Technologies Evaluated," *Ground Water Currents* (April 1995): 1, http://nepis.epa.gov (Accessed June 3, 2009).

Introduction

Before reading what follows, read the *introduction* in Figure 8.11. Have it in mind as you read this section.

An introduction *must do* these two things:

- Announce the subject of the report
- Announce the purpose of the report

An introduction *may do* any of these four things:

- Catch the reader's interest in the article or report
- Define terms and concepts
- Provide theoretical and historical background
- Forecast the content and organization of the report

INTRODUCTION

This document contains detailed information on how steam injection can be used to recover organic contaminants from the subsurface, the contaminant and subsurface conditions for which the process may be appropriate, and general design and equipment considerations. In addition, laboratory and field-scale experiments are described, and available treatment cost information is provided. This document is not meant to provide detailed information that would allow the design of a steam injection remediation project, but rather to provide design considerations to familiarize remediation workers with what is involved in the process.

FIGURE 8.11   Introduction to Journal Article

Source: Adapted from Eva L. Davis, "Steam Injection for Soil and Aquifer Remediation," *EPA: Ground Water Issue* (January 1998): 1, http://www.epa.gov/tio/tsp/download/steaminj.pdf (Accessed June 3, 2009).

How many of the optional things your introduction does depends on your audience and plan for your report or article. For a general, nontechnical audience, you would likely begin with something to catch the reader's interest. If your report or article uses words and concepts that the audience will need defined and explained in order to understand your subject matter, you may choose to provide the definitions and explanations in the introduction. However, you may also choose to provide them elsewhere in the article, perhaps where you first use each word or concept. The same holds true for providing needed theoretical and historical background.

If your report is complex, you would be wise to forecast its content and organization. For a short, uncomplicated report or article, you could probably forgo this step, but it is always appropriate to include it.

No matter what else you *may* do in your introduction, you *must* always announce your subject and purpose. In other words, tell your readers what you are talking about and why.

Introductions to articles aimed at general audiences tend to be interest-catching and more informal than introductions aimed at specialized audiences. In these general-audience introductions, the subject and purpose will be announced but perhaps somewhat indirectly. Figure 8.12 illustrates such an introduction. It asks questions to remind the reader that serious environmental problems still exist. Some inference is required of the reader, but it is clear that the subject will be a kind of pollution known rather awkwardly as *nonpoint source pollution,* and the purpose will be to describe where such pollution occurs and how it affects the environment.

Creating interest-catching introductions like the one in Figure 8.12 is appropriate for a general audience; just don't get too breathless about it.

Discussion

The *discussion,* where you fulfill your subject and purpose, will be the longest part of your article or report. How you organize and write it will depend on your purpose and audience. For direction, see Chapters 1–7 and remember the seven principles of technical writing:

1. Know your purpose and your writing situation.

2. Know your audience and their situation.

3. Choose and organize your content around your purpose and audience.

INTRODUCTION

Why is there still water that's too dirty for swimming, fishing, or drinking? Why are native species of plants and animals disappearing from many rivers, lakes, and coastal waters?

The United States has made tremendous advances in the past 25 years to clean up the aquatic environment by controlling pollution from industries and sewage treatment plants. Unfortunately, we did not do enough to control pollution from diffuse, or nonpoint, sources. Today, nonpoint source (NPS) pollution remains the Nation's largest source of water quality problems. It's the main reason that approximately 40 percent of our surveyed rivers, lakes, and estuaries are not clean enough to meet basic uses such as fishing or swimming.

NPS pollution occurs when rainfall, snowmelt, or irrigation runs over land or through the ground, picks up pollutants, and deposits them into rivers, lakes, and coastal waters or introduces them into ground water. Imagine the path taken by a drop of rain from the time it hits the ground to when it reaches a river, ground water, or the ocean. Any pollutant it picks up on its journey can become part of the nps problem. NPS pollution also includes adverse changes to the vegetation, shape, and flow of streams and other aquatic systems.

FIGURE 8.12   Introduction for a General Audience

Source: Nonpoint Source Pollution: The Nation's Largest Water Quality Problem 2008, http://www.epa.gov/nps/facts/point1.htm

4. Write clearly and precisely.
5. Use good page design.
6. Think visually.
7. Write ethically.

Conclusions and Recommendations

Analytical reports require *conclusions*. Recommendation reports require *conclusions* and *recommendations*. *Conclusions* are opinions based on the data in reports. For example, one journal article analyzed data that indicate that ulcers are caused by bacteria, not stress, as previously thought. The last paragraph of the article expressed a conclusion based on the data:

> Meanwhile, the future of current ulcer sufferers looks brighter than ever. Says consensus team member Ann L. B. Williams, M.D., of George Washington University Medical College, "We now have an opportunity to cure a disease that previously we had only been able to suppress or control."[2]

Whereas *conclusions* are opinions based on the data presented, *recommendations* are the actions recommended (or recommended against) based on the conclusions. Recommendation reports, often called *feasibility reports*, are common in business and government organizations. The studies that lead to such reports examine problems. For example, researchers working for a state prison system may be asked to look for ways to reduce the increasing pressure on prison facilities caused by growing prison populations. After due study, the researchers may reach a conclusion such as this one:

> A major conclusion, based on our data, is that society and nonviolent offenders might be better served by having such offenders perform community service over several years rather than serve prison terms. Removing nonviolent offenders from the prison population would help reduce the overcrowding that exists.

Based on such a conclusion, the researchers then make a recommendation, such as this:

> We recommend legislation allowing and encouraging judges to sentence nonviolent offenders to long-term community service, rather than prison. The legislation should authorize follow-up research to analyze the value of the community service and its effect on the recidivism rate of those sentenced to such service.

Because conclusions are opinions and because recommendations are based on conclusions, be sure the conclusions you reach are well grounded in reliable data.

If you have more than a few conclusions, you might help your reader by listing and even rating them, as is done in Figure 8.13.

CONCLUSIONS

The following conclusions are presented in approximate order of degree of certainty in the conclusion, based on the quality of the underlying database. The conclusions progress from those with greater certainty to those with lesser certainty.

- Conversion of mercury cell chlor-alkali plants to a mercury-free process is technically feasible and has been previously demonstrated.

- Energy conservation and switching to low-mercury fuels would reduce the amount of mercury being emitted by utility boilers.

- Injection of activated carbon into the flue gas of MWC's and MWI's can achieve mercury reductions of at least 85 percent. The addition of activated carbon to the flue gas of these source types would not have a significant impact on the amount of particulate matter requiring disposal.

- Numerous opportunities exist for replacing mercury in various products with other materials, such as solid state electronics for mercury switches, digital thermometers for mercury thermometers and zinc air batteries for mercury batteries.

- Removing mercury-containing products such as batteries, fluorescent lights and thermostats from the waste stream can reduce the mercury input to waste combustors without lowering the energy content of the waste stream. The mercury removal efficiency would vary, however, depending on the extent of the separation.

- Selenium filters are a demonstrated technology in Sweden for control of mercury emissions from lead smelters. Carbon filter beds have been used successfully in Germany for mercury control on utility boilers and MWC's. These technologies have not been demonstrated in the U.S.

- Control technologies designed for control of pollutants other than mercury (e.g., acid gases and particulate matter) vary in their mercury-removal capability, but in general achieve reductions no greater than 50 percent.

- The available data on coal cleaning indicate that mercury reductions ranged from zero to 64 percent. The average reduction was 21 percent. This variation may be due to several factors including different cleaning methods, different mercury concentrations in the raw coal and different mercury analytical techniques. There are no data available to assess the potential for mercury emissions from coal-cleaning slurries.

FIGURE 8.13   Conclusions Stated in List

Source: Office of Air Quality Planning and Standards and Office of Research and Development, *An Evaluation of Mercury Control Technology and Costs,* vol. 8 of *Mercury Study Report to Congress* (Washington, DC: U.S. Environmental Protection Agency, 1997), 6-1.

Appendixes

As their name indicates, *appendixes* are items appended to the main body of a report. They are excellent devices to help satisfy the needs of a dual audience for a report. For example, suppose the prison feasibility study described in the preceding section has two audiences: legislators and legislative aides. The legislators will want to know the salient facts and the conclusions and recommendations reached. They will not want to be buried under accounts of research methods and the like. However, the legislative aides may need such information to evaluate the study.

You can make two mistakes in selecting material for an appendix. You may segregate material in the appendix that everyone in your audience needs and wants and, therefore, run the risk of it being overlooked. Conversely, you may load your appendix with material that nobody needs or wants, increasing the bulk of your report but not its value. As always, let your audience and purpose guide you in reaching such decisions.

Documentation

If you have included any sources, either visual or textual, in your report, you must credit them. Use the guidelines in Chapter 7 to create your internal documentation and reference list.

Copyright

Copyright laws protect most published work, including text and graphics published on the Internet. Exceptions are most materials published by the United States government and state and local governments, which are normally not copyrighted.

If your work will be unpublished—for example, a student report—you must identify your sources, including Internet sources, but you do not need permission to use copyrighted material. In general, if you plan to publish your work, you must get permission from the copyright holders (usually, the publishers) to use figures, graphics, and extended quotations from copyrighted works. See *The Chicago Manual of Style* concerning copyright law.

ACTIVITIES

1. Use an Internet search engine to find two or three federal or state government reports. Compare their tables of contents. What elements of reports do you find in each? How would you describe their page layouts? Do they contain visuals? If so, how many and what kind?

2. Think about other courses you have taken. Which ones required you to write reports? What kinds of reports were they? What were the purposes of these reports? What elements, described in this chapter, did you include in them? How were these reports similar? How were they different?

CHAPTER ASSIGNMENTS

Assignment 1 for Individual Writers: Informal Report on Writing in the Workplace

The *Occupational Outlook Handbook* is a federal government publication that provides career information about hundreds of different kinds of jobs. The handbook is updated every two years. Your library will likely have one or more copies of the handbook, and it is available online at http://www.bls.gov/OCO/. Go to the *Occupational Outlook Handbook* and review the descriptions of jobs that interest you after graduation. What kinds of writing do people who have these jobs complete? Write a short informal report that answers this question.

Assignment 2 for a Writing Team: Oral Report on Writing in the Workplace

Complete the individual assignment in this chapter first. Then form teams based on similar occupational interests. Read and analyze your individual short informal reports on writing in the workplace. After you have read each other's reports, combine your findings into a single 5–10 minute oral report that describes the writing tasks individuals complete in the workplaces you have researched. Your oral report will have many of the same elements as a written report: opening summary of findings, introduction, discussion, and conclusion. If your classroom has electronic slide show technology available, create an electronic slide show to accompany your oral report. Your slide show should include visuals that support your findings. You might use images of reports or of individuals writing in the workplaces you're discussing. You and your teammates will need to work together to divide writing and presentation tasks.

9

Formats of Reports

Business and professional people write an assortment of reports. In these reports, they instruct, analyze information, propose work to be done, report progress on work, and report and interpret the results of research. This chapter suggests strategies and organizations for formatting a variety of reports.

Taken together, the elements used for any particular report make up its *format*. Despite seeming arbitrary at times, formats are quite functional. For the reader, they improve accessibility, selective reading, and comprehension. For the writer, formats aid in developing a report logically. Knowing what each element contributes to the report helps the writer to ensure that each element will be useful.

While these elements and the formats created from them are important to know, it is equally important for you to recognize that these suggestions are based on conventional or typical uses. They are not hard-and-fast structures that allow you to plug in the same information each time you write. Because each report writing situation is different, variations in these formats are not only possible but likely within specific workplaces. Knowing your specific audience, purpose, and situation will help you to modify these conventional formats to meet the needs of each assignment.

Instructions

Most instructions have a basic three-part format: an introduction, a list of equipment and materials needed, and how-to instructions. If you have ever followed a recipe in cooking or built a model airplane, the format will be immediately familiar to you. Many instructions also include warnings, theory, and a glossary.

Introduction

An introduction to instructions must announce the subject and purpose of the instructions, something like this:

> Leaking faucets waste water, stain the sink, and create annoying dripping sounds. With the right equipment, stopping the leak is a simple process.

This simple introduction makes clear that the subject is *stopping a faucet leak* and the purpose is to show readers how to do it. In addition, this introduction provides motivation for doing the task—stop waste, staining, and annoying sounds.

If the process you are going to describe is complex, you might also preview it:

> The process involves turning off the water to the faucet, disassembling the faucet, replacing the faucet washer, reassembling the faucet, and turning the water on again.

You may also include information such as warnings, references to a glossary, and definitions, but in general, keep introductions uncomplicated.

List of Equipment and Materials

People about to do a task need to know what they must have to complete the task. A list detailing the needed equipment and materials provides the necessary information:

- A box of washers of assorted sizes
- A screwdriver
- An adjustable wrench

How much information you provide in your list depends on your audience analysis. If your analysis tells you that your readers are experienced tool users, the simple list above should be sufficient. For inexperienced tool users, you may have to expand the list:

- A screwdriver of the appropriate type and size. Screws have either straight-blade slots or phillips slots (see

Figure 1). The screwdriver must match the slot. In either
case, the screwdriver blade must fit securely into the
slot of the screw without slippage (see Figure 2).

As this expanded list indicates, figures (not shown here) make clear the
distinction between a straight-blade slot and a phillips slot and how the
screwdriver blade should fit the slot. As Chapter 6, Think Visually, emphasizes, when pictures are clearer than words, use pictures.

Sometimes, you may find that your readers need a rather complete
description of a tool or mechanism involved in a process. In describing
mechanisms or tools, you can include information on their purpose and
function, parts and subparts, purpose and function of the parts and subparts, construction, materials, appearance, size, color, and so forth. You
can also describe how to use the mechanism safely. How much of this
sort of information you include depends, as always, on what your readers actually need. Figure 9.1 (p. 126) provides a good example of such a
description. Again, notice the use of illustrations in the description.

If you think it is necessary, you can also include information
about where materials and equipment can be obtained, what they cost,
and so forth. Tell your readers what they need to know to do the job
properly.

How-To Instructions

Figure 9.2 (p. 127) illustrates a partial list of how-to instructions. Look at
it now, before you continue with the text. As Figure 9.2 demonstrates,
how-to instructions follow these principles:

- Present each instruction of process separately and in chronological
  order.

- Use simple language, active voice, and imperative mood: "Loosen
  packing nut with wrench."

- Use clarifying illustrations.

- Include helpful advice: "Most nuts loosen by turning counter-
  clockwise."

Although how-to instructions are not always numbered (as in Figure 9.2),
they frequently are.

Portable Power Circular Saws

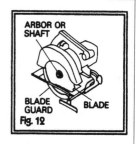

The portable power circular saw can save you "muscle power" and time (fig. 12). You can rent or buy one. It may be used as a crosscut saw or a ripsaw—depending upon the type of blade used.

The *saw blade* should be adjusted so that the amount of blade that extends below the "shoe" is slightly greater (1/16 to 1/8 inch) than the thickness of material to be cut. As you guide the saw forward, the blade is exposed for cutting (fig. 13).

For ripping work, circular saws come with a "ripping guide." After adjusting the blade, set the ripping guide the same distance from the saw as the width of the material to be cut off.

Then place the guide against the edge of the piece as you cut (fig. 14).

For crosscutting, or cutting off material, turn the ripping guide upside down, so that it will be out of the way. Using a framing square and pencil, draw a line to mark where to cut. Then guide the saw blade carefully along the line.

Using a portable power saw can save much time and effort. For safety and the proper use of the saw, follow these steps:

1. Make sure that the saw you use is equipped with a guard that will automatically adjust in use so that none of the teeth are exposed above the work.
2. Make sure the saw is equipped with an automatic power cutoff button.
3. Always wear goggles or face mask when using a power saw.
4. Carefully examine the material and make certain that it is free of nails or other metal before you start cutting.
5. Grasp the saw with both hands and hold it firmly against the work.
6. Never overload the saw motor by pushing too hard or cutting material that is too thick for this small saw.
7. Always try to make a straight cut to keep from binding the saw blade. If it does bind, back the saw out slowly and firmly in a straight line. As you continue with the cutting, adjust the direction of the cut so that you are cutting in a straight line.
8. Always pull the electric plug before you make any adjustments to the saw or inspect the blade.

FIGURE 9.1   Mechanism Description

Source: U.S. Department of Agriculture, *Simple Home Repairs: Outside* (Washington, DC: GPO, 1986), 6.

It is critically important in writing how-to instructions to break the process down into manageable steps. An instruction may include only one step (as in instruction 3 in Figure 9.2) or several (as in instructions 1 and 2). When you include more than one step in an instruction, be sure they are all closely related.

If you are experienced in the process being described, you may unintentionally leave out steps that you have come to do almost automatically, without thinking about them. Be sure to think through the entire process, step by step; leave out nothing that your audience analysis tells you your reader needs. A good check is to ask someone of the skill level you expect in your audience to perform the process following your instructions. Gaps in your instructions will show up quickly.

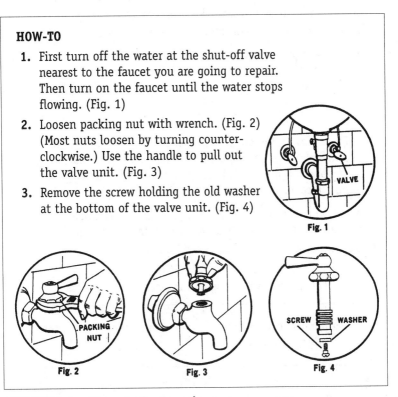

HOW-TO

1. First turn off the water at the shut-off valve nearest to the faucet you are going to repair. Then turn on the faucet until the water stops flowing. (Fig. 1)

2. Loosen packing nut with wrench. (Fig. 2) (Most nuts loosen by turning counter-clockwise.) Use the handle to pull out the valve unit. (Fig. 3)

3. Remove the screw holding the old washer at the bottom of the valve unit. (Fig. 4)

FIGURE 9.2   How-to Instructions

Source: U.S. Department of Agriculture, *Simple Home Repairs: Inside* (Washington, DC: GPO, 1986), 1.

Warnings

To protect consumers from injury and to protect companies from expensive lawsuits, warnings are given extensively in instructions. They may stand out in a separate section of their own or be part of the introduction, list of equipment and materials, or how-to instructions. Manufacturers have learned (to their sorrow) that risks that seem obvious to them are not obvious to everyone. Err on the side of too many warnings, not too few.

Make your warnings stand out so that no one will miss them. Box them; use a larger, distinctive, or different-colored typeface; use symbols, such as an exclamation point or a skull and crossbones. When the risk involved might lead to death or serious injury, use all three techniques.

Although there is not complete agreement on levels of warnings, three levels have become common: *Caution, Warning,* and *Danger:*

- Use *Caution* to warn against actions that may lead to undesirable results but that are not likely to damage equipment or injure people:

Caution

If you have external devices, such as an external hard drive, connected to your computer, turn them on before you turn on your computer. Failure to do so may keep your computer from recognizing them when you do turn them on.

- Use *Warning* to warn against actions that may damage equipment or materials or cause mild injury to users:

> **WARNING**
> This process will erase all information on this disk.

- Use *Danger* to warn against actions that may result in serious injury or death:

> **DANGER!**
> Do not stand on the top two steps or the top of this stepladder. Doing so may result in a fall that could cause serious injury or death.

Theory

Sometimes, users of instructions may benefit from knowing the theory that underlies the instructions. Knowing the theory may clarify the procedures described or motivate users to follow the instructions. In the following example, the author of instructions meant for managers of seedling nurseries explains the theory underlying the instructions:

> Managers of container seedling nurseries sow multiple seeds per cell to increase the probability of having at least one germinant per cell. This ensures that their greenhouses are fully stocked so that seedling contracts may be filled. However, this practice wastes valuable seed and necessitates thinning extra germinants at an additional cost. Multiple sowing, therefore, should be minimized.
>
> Many factors influence how many seeds per cell to sow, including species, seed size, seed availability and cost, type and accuracy of sowing equipment, sowing and thinning labor costs, and germination data reliability. The primary factor, however, is greenhouse germination percentage. When germination percentage is known or assumed, nursery managers use various rules of thumb or rely on the probability tables found in Tinus and McDonald (1979) to determine the number of expected empty cells. These tables are complete but sometimes cumbersome and currently unavailable to new managers.
>
> Fortunately, the percentage of empty cells can be obtained using a hand-held calculator (Schwartz 1993). Taking this procedure one step farther, the probability tables of Tinus and McDonald (1979), showing both filled and empty cells, can be recreated on a personal computer.[1]

If the theory you present is lengthy, you may want to put it in a section by itself. Most of the time, however, you will present theory as part of your introduction, as in the previous example. Include theory in instructions only if you are reasonably sure your readers will benefit from it.

Glossary

Occasionally, you will use enough words that are unfamiliar to your readers to justify including a glossary with your instructions. When this is the case, construct your glossary following the instructions on pages 108–110.

You may place your glossary at the beginning or at the end of your instructions. In either case, refer the reader to it in your introduction.

Analytical Reports

Analytical reports analyze data to arrive at conclusions. Some reports go one step further and recommend that actions be taken or not taken, based on the conclusions reached. If the person making the report has the authority to do so, the report might state a decision. Therefore, analytical reports may also be known as *recommendation reports* or *decision reports*. When the purpose of the report is to examine the feasibility of some plan of action, it may also be called a *feasibility report*.

The executives of organizations are constantly making decisions based on answers to questions such as these:

> What can be done about the high absentee rate in our Charleston plant?
>
> What is the sales potential of our new VCR?
>
> Which health plan should we choose for our company?

The answers to such questions are most often given in analytical reports. When the report is simple and short, it is usually presented in a memorandum or letter. (These types of reports are discussed in Chapter 10, Formats of Correspondence.) When the report is complex and long, it needs more structure, such as a title page, table of contents, and summary. These additional elements are not included to increase the weight and formality of the report; rather, they are included to help readers find their way through the report. (Chapter 8, Elements of Reports, provides the information you need to construct the elements of long reports. Here, the discussion is about how to put the elements into an appropriate format.)

Format

Depending on your purpose, the needs of your readers, and the content itself, analytical reports will use formats such as the following:

Format I	**Format II**
Title page	Title page
Table of contents	Table of contents
Executive summary	Introduction
Introduction	Summary
Discussion	Conclusions
Conclusions	Recommendations
Recommendations	Discussion

In Format I, although the executive summary highlights major conclusions and recommendations, the emphasis falls on the discussion. In Format II, the discussion is de-emphasized and the summary, conclusions, and recommendations are brought to the forefront.

Both are good formats. The one you choose would depend on your needs and those of your readers. For example, you might know that your readers will be skeptical of your conclusions and, therefore, wish to emphasize your discussion by choosing Format I. Or you might know that your readers will prefer seeing the big picture first and, therefore, choose Format II. To formats like these, you can add, as needed, elements such as lists of illustrations, glossaries, documentation, and appendixes (all explained in Chapter 8, Elements of Reports).

Discussion sections of analytical reports can be rather specialized, depending on the questions being examined. The following should help you sort things out.

Discussion Sections

Discussion sections in analytical reports tend to use one of the following organizations: *classical argument, pro and con, choice of alternatives,* or *problem/solution.* No matter which organization you choose, your discussion has to build a firm base for the conclusions, recommendations, and decisions that follow from it.

In a *classical argument* format, you would support a large opinion by a series of smaller opinions, which are in turn supported by facts. In argument, the large opinion is called the *major premise;* the smaller opinions are called *minor premises*. Your discussion format might look like this:

Major premise

> Minor premise A
>
> > *Factual support*
>
> Minor premise B
>
> > *Factual support*
>
> Minor premise C
>
> > *Factual support*

In an actual argument, your format might look like this:

> Fusion energy has the potential to be a major source of energy in the twenty-first century.

- Fuel for fusion energy is easily available and virtually inexhaustible.

  Factual support

- Fusion energy does not produce the pollutants that lead to global warming.

  Factual support

- Fusion energy is a safer source of power than present-day nuclear power plants.

  Factual support[2]

Other forms of argument are all variations of the classical argument format.

If existing opinions and facts weigh against the major premise, it is both ethical and convincing to use a *pro and con* argument. (*Ethical* because you are not hiding anything. *Convincing* because you are perceived not to be hiding anything.) A pro and con argument weighs the points in favor of something (*pros*) against the points opposed (*cons*), resulting in this format:

A statement or a question

> *Pro:*   Opinions and facts supporting the affirmative
>
> *Con:*   Opinions and facts supporting the negative

An actual pro and con argument might break out like this:

> Fusion energy has the potential to be a major source of energy in the twenty-first century.

Pros

- Fuel for fusion energy is easily available and virtually inexhaustible.

  Factual support

- Fusion energy does not produce the pollutants that lead to global warming.

  Factual support

- Fusion energy is a safer source of power than present-day nuclear power plants.

  Factual support

Cons

- Although fusion energy is safer than fission energy, it does produce high-energy neutrons that induce radioactivity, leaving problems of radioactive waste.

  Factual support

- The cost of fusion energy is too high for it to be a practical source of power.

  Factual support

Even if you think the *pro* side of the argument is the right side, to present an ethical argument, you should still include the *cons*. However, it is perfectly ethical to point out ways in which mitigating facts or circumstances weaken the *con* side. For example, evidence suggests that, with the right technology, the cost of fusion energy could be comparable to that of fossil fuels.

After weighing the pros and cons for your readers, you will be expected, of course, to arrive at a conclusion: Fusion energy has the potential to be a major source of energy in the twenty-first century. Yes or no?

Frequently, an analytical discussion calls for a *choice of alternatives*. You might be called on to make a recommendation concerning some major company purchase—for example, vans to make company deliveries. In a choice of alternatives plan, you have to deal with the alternatives available and the criteria by which you judge the alternatives. *Criteria* are the standards you use to judge something. In the case of vans, you might have as alternatives all the vans made by major truck manufacturers. The criteria might concern initial cost, operating cost, carrying capacity, and maintenance record. You can organize your discussion by either alternatives or criteria:

By Alternatives	By Criteria
Van A	Initial cost
Initial cost	Van A
Operating cost	Van B
Carrying capacity	Operating cost
Maintenance record	Van A
Van B	Van B
Initial cost	Carrying capacity
Operating cost	Van A
Carrying capacity	Van B
Maintenance record	Maintenance record
	Van A
	Van B

Organizing by alternatives has the advantage of offering a complete discussion of each van in one section. Organizing by criteria has the advantage of allowing for selective reading; that is, some readers may be more interested in cost than carrying capacity. Organizing by criteria allows them to find and read the section they are most concerned with. Both plans are good. As usual, your purpose and audience will help you choose the one best suited to your situation.

In the first part of a *problem/solution* discussion, you define the problem. Use the available data to demonstrate that a problem really exists. For example, suppose you are an executive with a computer company that has a problem with its technical help line. Customers who call it get repeated busy signals. And after connecting to the help line, they may have waits up to an hour. To define the problem, you answer questions like these:

Typically, how many times does a buyer of one of your computers call in seeking help?

How many calls a day does your help line receive?

How many technical support consultants does the company have?

What is the cost to your company of running the help line?

Can the company afford to increase the service to an acceptable level and keep its profit margin high enough to stay in business?

How is the problem damaging customer relations?

and so forth

After you define the problem, offer your solution. If there are criteria you must apply to any solution, clearly state them. For example, in the technical help line problem, a criterion might be that the solution must be affordable to the company. A solution that cut too heavily into company profit margins—such as hiring large numbers of consultants—would not be acceptable. Perhaps in this case, your solution might be to allow calls only to customers who buy service policies with their computers. The money from the service policies would pay for an expanded and acceptable technical help line.

After stating your solution, you would need to demonstrate its likely effectiveness. Again, you would be using your data to answer questions:

Have other companies tried this approach?

How successful have they been?

How much money is needed to expand the help line to an acceptable level of service?

How much would a service policy have to cost?

How would consumers react to buying such a policy?

and so forth

Your discussion has to show the strong likelihood of your solution being successful.

If you offer more than one solution, the solution portion of the report might use a choice of alternatives plan. In this case, you might offer two alternatives: a service policy and pay-as-you-go. In the pay-as-you-go plan, the customer would pay for each help call made. You might then compare the alternatives using criteria such as customer acceptance, ease of administration, and effect on profit margin. At the end of your discussion, you could weigh the evidence in a series of conclusions and recommend which solution the company should choose.

Using the various forms of argument to analyze a set of facts, you can carefully build a powerful case for your position. But remember that, ultimately, your analysis can be no better than your facts. Also remember that, even though you may be trying to convince your readers to accept your point of view, it is your responsibility to argue ethically. Do not, for example, slant your facts one way or the other.

Proposals

In a proposal, one organization (or sometimes an individual) offers, for a price, its services to another organization. For example, Organization X, a research organization, may offer to research and present a solution to a problem that Organization Y has. Or Company A, a computer software manufacturer, may offer to research the software needs of Company B and then to install the necessary software. A *proposal* is essentially a specialized form of argument and uses many of the techniques discussed in the previous section.

Proposals are either *solicited* or *unsolicited.* In a solicited proposal, an organization in need of services advertises its needs in a document called a *request for proposal* (*RFP*). The RFP will state the organization's needs and request proposals that can satisfy those needs. The RFP will usually state quite specifically the format that proposals must take, sometimes right down to the headings to be used. When this is the case, follow the instructions given in the RFP point by point. Failure to do so will likely result in a rejected proposal.

In an unsolicited proposal, an organization sees a problem that another organization has and offers to provide the solution through its services. The following section describes a format that could be used in an unsolicited proposal, and the section following that one describes a format that a student could use to propose a project to an instructor.

Unsolicited Proposals

Short proposals may look like correspondence. Longer proposals may need title pages, tables of contents, and so forth (all described in Chapter 8, Elements of Reports). In either case, the central format of the proposal will look something like this:

Project summary

Project description

    Introduction

    Rationale and significance

    Plan of work

    Facilities and equipment

Personnel

Budget

Appendixes

A *project summary* is essentially an executive summary (see pp. 111–114). In it, you briefly summarize your proposed services and emphasize the objectives of your proposal. Be sure to highlight how meeting those objectives will satisfy the needs of the client organization.

A *project description* comprises six sections: (1) introduction, (2) rationale and significance, (3) plan of work, (4) facilities and equipment, (5) personnel, and (6) budget.

1. Be sure your *introduction* (see pp. 115–116) makes clear the services you are proposing and how the successful outcome of your proposal will benefit your proposed client.

2. In the *rationale and significance* section, define the problem and make clear the need for a solution, describe the solution, show that the solution is feasible, and explain the benefits of the solution. This section has the characteristics of an analytical report (see pp. 130–136).

3. To carry out your solution, you must have a *plan of work*. A plan of work section includes smaller elements that state the scope, describe the methodology, break the work into its component tasks, and schedule the work:

- Describe the scope of the work to be done; that is, make clear what you will do and, sometimes, what you will not do. Carefully describing scope may prevent later difficulties with clients who expect work that they think you have promised.

- Describe your methodology. For example, will your research define the problem you perceive in the organization? If so, what methods will you use? Will you, perhaps, use focus groups and questionnaires? If so, how will you evaluate the results you obtain through these methods? Show your potential clients that you know what you are doing.

■ The proposed work can no doubt be broken down into smaller tasks. For example, you may first give a test questionnaire to a small group. After evaluating the results, you may modify the questionnaire and give it to all the client's employees. Next, you may evaluate the results, and so on.

When you have made your work plan and its component tasks clear, give the schedule for completion of that plan. You may find a flowchart, showing the tasks in relation to the time it will take to accomplish them, useful for clarifying your schedule.

4. In the *facilities and equipment* section, tell your prospective clients what facilities and equipment you will need and how you plan to get access to them. Answer questions like these: If you need a certain kind of laboratory, do you already have the use of it? Do you have the equipment needed? If not, how do you plan to get it? Who will pay for it, you or the client? If the client will pay, will you use this equipment exclusively for that client? If not, how big a share must the client pay? You have a legal as well as an ethical responsibility to state clearly the answers to such questions.

5. In the *personnel* section, list the people who will work on the project if the proposal is accepted. Give details of their relevant education and experience, such as the dates of past projects of a similar nature, the names and addresses of previous clients, and publications in the field of the proposal. The more detailed you can be about relevant qualifications, the better the chance of your proposal being accepted.

6. Finally, present your *budget*. In a table or list of some sort, itemize your costs. If you have an extensive budget, you may need a classification scheme—for example, equipment, laboratory costs, salaries, travel, fees, and so forth.

In addition to these six sections, you may need *appendixes* to your project description (see p. 120). Appendixes may include additional budget information, biographical information, company background, histories of earlier successful projects, and so forth. In making your selection, remember that your proposal is a sales document that is being read by busy people. They will read relevant appendixes but may ignore anything that appears to be boilerplate.

Student Proposals

Students frequently must propose projects of various sorts to their instructors. For instance, a student in an advanced biology class may have to propose a semester-long experiment. A student in a writing class may have to propose a project such as a feasibility report. If you are a student, and an instructor gives you a plan for the proposal, follow it carefully. In the absence of such instructions, a scaled-down version of the unsolicited proposal will be appropriate. The following is an accepted format:

- Combined executive summary (see pp. 111–114) and introduction (see pp. 115–116) that makes clear the subject, purpose, scope, and benefits of the project
- Task and time schedule
- Resources needed and where they are available
- Your qualifications for carrying out the project

Progress Reports

If you are working for a client, he or she has a natural interest in the answer to the question: How are you doing? Progress reports are designed to answer that question. Some work, particularly work that results from an accepted proposal, requires progress reports at stated intervals, perhaps monthly. Whether written according to schedule or at irregular intervals, progress reports follow fairly standard formats.

What follows is one such format. Like all reports, if it is only a few pages long, write the progress report as a memo or letter. If it is long and involved, add title pages and the like, as needed.

Introduction Use a standard introduction (see pp. 115–116). Make clear what work you are reporting.

Project Description In a project description, briefly describe the work being done, clearly stating its purpose and scope. The scope statement breaks the work down into its component tasks—for example, devise questionnaires, administer questionnaires, evaluate questionnaire results, write final report.

Work Completed Tell the reader what you have accomplished to date. In a long-running project that requires several progress reports covering several periods, you might divide this section further as follows:

> Summary of work accomplished in preceding periods
>
> Work accomplished in reporting period

You may further subdivide these sections by the tasks you have indicated in your scope statement, like this:

> Work accomplished in reporting period:
>> Devising questionnaires
>> Administering questionnaires
>> Evaluating questionnaires
>> Writing final report

Work Planned for Future Periods Tell the reader what you expect to accomplish in the future: your goals, expected outcomes, and schedule for achieving these goals. You might organize the information as identified below:

> Work planned for next period
>
> Work planned for future periods

Appraisal of Progress Evaluate your progress. Indicate where you are ahead of schedule and where you are behind. Don't offer a litany of excuses, but if there are good reasons as to why the work is not going according to plan, state them clearly. The executive summary (see pp. 111–114) is a good model for this appraisal.

As in all writing, don't complicate your progress reports any more than necessary, but do answer thoroughly a client's three basic questions:

1. How are you doing?
2. What have you done?
3. What are you going to do next?

Empirical Research Reports

If you pursue a scientific career, you will frequently have to report the results of your empirical research. The format of an empirical research report closely parallels the stages of the scientific method. Scientists typically start with questions for which they want answers. They then review the literature to see if other scientists have asked the same or similar questions. If the specific questions have not been answered, the scientists devise methods to get at the answers, often by revising previously reported research. When the results of the research are in, scientists analyze them in light of previous research to see what they mean and to arrive at conclusions. Because the overall format of the research report follows their research patterns so well, scientists find it easy to organize their research reports. The major components of an empirical research report are as follows:

> Abstract
>
> Introduction
>
> Literature Review
>
> Materials and Methods
>
> Results
>
> Discussion
>
> Conclusions

Abstract

The abstract summarizes key points of the report, including objectives of the research, major results, and conclusions. After reading it, the reader will know the objective of the research, why the research was conducted, the major results, the meaning of the results, and the major conclusions of the author. The reader now has many options: read the entire report, read only the discussion to see how the author analyzes the results, check out the conclusions, and so forth. The reader's knowledge, needs, and interests, not the author's, govern the options chosen.

Introduction

The introduction describes the subject, scope, significance, and objectives of the research.

Literature Review

The literature review summarizes previous research that has bearing on the research being reported. Such research may address objectives, materials and methods, and the rationale for the work done. To learn and understand, readers have to be led from the known to the unknown—that which is to be learned. Most formats allow for this logical progression. In the case of the empirical research report, the introduction and literature review together serve this purpose. By reviewing past research in the field, the literature review provides the necessary background to understand the objective of the research, the need for the research, and the techniques used in the research.

With this new knowledge, the reader can follow the descriptions of the materials and methods used in the research. With materials and methods understood, the reader can comprehend the results they achieved. With all the preceding known, the reader can follow the analysis of the results and understand the conclusions.

The progression from the known to the unknown also supports selective reading. For instance, the reader may already know the background and techniques of the immediate research well. Such knowledge allows the reader to move directly to the results and discussion.

In journal articles, the literature review is most often integrated with the introduction. In dissertations, the literature review usually stands by itself with its own heading.

Materials and Methods

The materials and methods section may describe any of the following: the design of the research, the materials used, the procedures followed, or the methods used for observation and evaluation. An experienced researcher in the field should be able to replicate the research using this section as a guide.

Results

The results section is a factual accounting of what the researcher has found. Writers of research reports make extensive use of tables and graphs in the results section.

Discussion

The discussion section is an analytical discussion that interprets the results (see pp. 116–117). It answers questions such as these: Were the research objectives met? If not, why not? How well do the results correlate with results from previous research? If they do not correlate well, why not? What future work should follow this research? In many formats, the results and discussion are combined.

Conclusions

If the researcher's conclusions are not integrated into the discussion, they are stated here.

ACTIVITIES

1. Almost every mechanical or digital product on the market is sold with instructions or a manual. Often consumers can also access instructions (including manuals) on the Internet. Examine the instructions or manuals for several products, and compare their contents, layouts, and visuals. What conclusions can you draw about how instructions and manuals are written? Support your answers with examples from the instructions you have examined.

2. Many times instructions or manuals seem incomplete and even useless to consumers. The classic example of this problem occurs when someone tries to use a software manual to solve a problem and spends more time looking for an answer than applying it. Think about problems you have encountered with manuals, describe them, and discuss how better planning, writing, and design could improve poor instruction writing.

3. Wordless instructions that rely entirely on graphics to illustrate tasks to be completed are increasing in popularity, especially among corporations that manufacture and distribute their products internationally. These instructions use numbers but few, if any, words to relay directions to readers. If possible, find examples of wordless in-

structions (at home or on the Internet), bring the example to class, and discuss the advantages and disadvantages of instructing with pictures rather than words.

CHAPTER ASSIGNMENTS

Assignment 1 for Individual Writers: Proposal

Proposals respond to a need. They offer to produce or sell something to meet that need. In this assignment, you will write a proposal to help someone do something. Specifically, your proposal should provide help or instructions for completing a task. Your proposal should be written to your instructor, asking permission to write the instructions. You may choose any task, serious or fun, such as playing a game, using a a tool, or working with a kitchen appliance. If you have completed the individual and team assignments in Chapters 1–7, you might propose a set of instructions for using the groupware your team recommended. Use the guidelines in this chapter to identify report elements to include in your proposal.

Assignment 2 for a Writing Team: Instructions

Divide into teams of two or three and write an instruction set. If your class has completed the individual proposal assignments, choose the approved proposal project your team would most like to complete. Use the guidelines in this chapter to help you plan, organize, and write your proposal. Use page layout strategies that help readers use instructions, and include visuals to help readers see how to complete tasks in the instruction set.

10

Formats of Correspondence

Letters are used for correspondence outside an organization. *Memorandums* (or *memos*) are used for correspondence within an organization.

Letters and memos may (and in some cases should) contain many of the elements found in more formal reports (as described in Chapter 8, Elements of Reports). That is, they may contain introductions, summaries (particularly executive summaries), discussions, conclusions, and recommendations. However, these elements may be somewhat abbreviated. They also may be labeled differently—"Findings" or "Discussion," for instance—or have substantive headings, such as "Existing Patient Populations." Such labeling is particularly appropriate for letters and memos that substitute for longer, more formal reports.

Shorter letters and memos that convey information or opinions, make complaints, answer complaints, and so forth may have simple introductions and perhaps even summaries, but will not label them as such.

The first section of this chapter deals with the formal elements used in standard letters. The second, third, and fourth sections deal with some important stylistic elements in simplified letters, memos, and e-mails. The closing section describes the correspondence used in a job hunt: résumés and letters of application.

Formal Elements of Letters

One of the disadvantages of having a personal computer on every desk is that executives in middle management are sometimes responsible for producing their own correspondence. Therefore, the formal elements of correspondence may be more important to you than you would like to believe. Also, good page design (see Chapter 5) is as important in letters as in reports.

Figure 10.1 illustrates a well-formatted business letter. The following sections explain the components found in such letters.

Letterhead

On the job, you will likely have a printed letterhead on your stationery, containing your organization's address, telephone and fax numbers, and e-mail address. Figure 10.1 (pp. 147–148) shows a typical printed letterhead. If you don't have a printed letterhead, as might be the case when you are job hunting, simply place your address flush left, as illustrated in Figure 10.8 (p. 162). A more sophisticated technological solution for creating a letterhead is to use word-processing or image editing software to create a letterhead or letterhead graphic that you can insert into the header of your document. Creating your own letterhead can be fun, and it personalizes your correspondence and gives it a professional appearance.

Notice that standard postal abbreviations are used for states and provinces (see Figure 10.2, p. 149). However, words such as *Street, Road,* and so forth are not abbreviated.

Date Line

Use one of these two styles for date lines: *16 March 2009* or *March 16, 2009.* Notice that the month is not abbreviated and number suffixes, such as *th* and *nd,* are not used.

Inside Address

Place the name and address of the person receiving the letter four spaces below the date line. Use a courtesy title, such as *Ms.* or *Professor,* with the name. The abbreviations *Mr., Ms.,* and *Dr.* are standard usage. Other

BROWER CONSTRUCTION COMPANY

1998 Lee Highway
Freedom, MO 63032
Phone: 314-555-6788
Fax: 314-555-3097
E-mail: browercon@west.net

July 27, 2008

Mrs. Irma Weaver
2 Brightside Lane
Freedom, MO 63032

Re: Your letter of July 17, 2008

Subject: Proposed solution of underground tank problem

Dear Mrs. Weaver:

We regret the installation of the underground oil tank on your property when we built your house. We did, indeed, receive the notice from the town clerk about the new city ordinance prohibiting underground oil tanks for environmental reasons. Unfortunately, for some reason, the news about the ordinance did not reach our design team in time.

However, the town clerk tells us that during the winter everyone with a building permit received a notice of the new ordinance. Your permit number was 615002. Apparently, you overlooked the notice, as did we.

(continued)

FIGURE 10.1   Standard Business Letter

Page 2
Mrs. Irma Weaver
27 July 2008

I think we have a shared responsibility in this matter, and neither of us should bear the full cost. Let me suggest the following: We will remove the underground tank and fittings, close off and seal the opening in your foundation, and fill the hole at no labor or material cost to you. We will charge you labor costs for installing an indoor tank and the difference between the price of the outside tank and the new indoor tank. Your total cost will be $420.34.

If this arrangement is satisfactory to you, please call and we'll schedule the work. We regret any inconvenience you and Mr. Weaver have experienced and hope you will continue to enjoy your new house.

Sincerely yours,

Howard Brower

Howard Brower
Chief Operating Officer

HB: pgc

Encl. Copy of town clerk's letter to building permit holders

FIGURE 10.1 (*continued*)

courtesy titles, such as *Professor* and *Captain,* are spelled out. When you use the courtesy title *Dr.* before the name, do not use the equivalent (for example, *Ph.D.*) after the name. Put a one-word job title, such as *Director,* after the name. Place a job title of two or more words on the next line after the name.

United States				Canada	
Alabama	AL	Missouri	MO	Alberta	AB
Alaska	AK	Montana	MT	British Columbia	BC
American		Nebraska	NE	Labrador	LB
Samoa	AS	Nevada	NV	Manitoba	MB
Arizona	AZ	New Hampshire	NH	New Brunswick	NB
Arkansas	AR	New Jersey	NJ	Newfoundland	NF
California	CA	New Mexico	NM	Nova Scotia	NS
Colorado	CO	New York	NY	Northwest	
Connecticut	CT	North Carolina	NC	Territories	NT
Delaware	DE	North Dakota	ND	Ontario	ON
District of		Ohio	OH	Prince Edward	
Columbia	DC	Oklahoma	OK	Island	PE
Florida	FL	Oregon	OR	Quebec (Province	
Georgia	GA	Pennsylvania	PA	de Quebec)	PQ
Guam	GU	Puerto Rico	PR	Saskatchewan	SK
Hawaii	HI	Rhode Island	RI	Yukon Territory	YT
Idaho	ID	South Carolina	SC		
Illinois	IL	South Dakota	SD		
Indiana	IN	Tennessee	TN		
Iowa	IA	Texas	TX		
Kansas	KS	Utah	UT		
Kentucky	KY	Vermont	VT		
Louisiana	LA	Virginia	VA		
Maine	ME	Virgin Islands	VI		
Maryland	MD	Washington	WA		
Massachusetts	MA	West Virginia	WV		
Michigan	MI	Wisconsin	WI		
Minnesota	MN	Wyoming	WY		
Mississippi	MS				

FIGURE 10.2   State, Territory, and Province Abbreviations for the United States and Canada

As in the letterhead, abbreviate names of states and provinces but not words like *Street*. Write the names of organizations and people exactly as they do. Use *Inc.,* not *Incorporated,* if the company does. Use *F. Xavier Jones,* not *Frank X. Jones,* if he does.

Re Line

The *Re* in the *re* line stands for "reference." Generally, the reference is to other documents, as in *Your letter of 12 April 2009* or *Your contract with Smith Brothers, dated 16 May 2009.*

Subject Line

In a subject line, you tell the reader what subject will be dealt with in your letter—for example, *Summer Schedule for Executive Committee Meetings.* Sometimes, the word *Subject* is used in the subject line, as in Figure 10.1. When *Subject* is omitted, the subject line generally appears in all capital letters, as in Figure 10.3.

Salutation

For the most part, writers still adhere to tradition and begin salutations with *Dear.* Follow *Dear* with the name used in the inside address—*Dear Ms. Pleasant* and so forth. Use a colon after the salutation, and place it as shown in Figure 10.1.

If you do not have a name to use, you have one of two choices: If it is an important letter—a proposal, for instance—get a name, even if it takes a long-distance phone call to do so. If it is a routine letter—such as an inquiry—use a simplified letter, as shown in Figure 10.3.

Body

Keep body paragraphs short, rarely more than six or seven lines, and space them as indicated in Figures 10.1 and 10.3. Do not split words between lines. Also do not split dates or names; that is, *February 11, 2009* should be on one line, as should *Margaret M. Briand.*

Complimentary Close

In most business correspondence, use a simple complimentary close, such as *Sincerely yours.* For correspondence with a friend, closes such as *Best regards* are suitable. Follow the close with a comma, and place it as in Figure 10.1.

BROWER CONSTRUCTION COMPANY

1998 Lee Highway
Freedom, MO 63032
Phone: 314-555-6788
Fax: 314-555-3097
E-mail: browercon@west.net

26 March 2008

Director, Corporate Research and Engineering
Burnham, Inc.
3660 Folwell Drive
Minneapolis, MN 55418

SPREAD-SPECTRUM HOME SECURITY SYSTEMS

Our company installs a good many Burnham Home Security Systems in the new homes we construct. These systems are hard wired, which presents no problems in new construction. However, increasingly, we are asked to provide security systems in existing homes. Here, hard wiring presents problems for which the only solution is running wires through walls, with all the accompanying expense.

I understand that Burnham is working on wireless security systems using a spread-spectrum modulation technique that will allow radio-frequency communication between the components of a home security system.

How far along is your research on this new system? Do you have a target date for marketing it? When it is ready, we will certainly consider it for use in both new construction and existing homes.

Howard Brower

Howard Brower
Chief Operating Officer
HB: pgc

FIGURE 10.3   Simplified Letter

Signature Block

Four spaces below the complimentary close, type your name and, if you have one, your title. To avoid complicating the life of a correspondent who doesn't know you, use enough of your name to indicate your gender. That is, use *Patrick M. Fields,* not *Pat Fields* or *P. M. Fields.* In the space between the complimentary close and your typed name, sign your name—legibly, please.

End Notations

Notations following the signature block indicate identification, enclosures, and copies (see Figure 10.1).

Identification In this type of notation, the writer's initials are in capital letters and the administrative assistant's initials are in lowercase:

FDR/hrc

Enclosures Enclosure lines indicate to the reader—sometimes in a general way, sometimes specifically—that you have enclosed additional material with your letter, as in the following two examples:

Enclosures (3)

Encl: Schedule for summer meetings

Copy In a copy line, you tell your correspondent who else is receiving a copy of the letter:

cc. Dr. Georgia Brown
    Mr. Hugh Binns

Continuation Page

When your letter exceeds one page, you need a continuation page or pages (see Figure 10.1). Follow these rules when constructing a continuation page:

- Use paper of the same color and weight as your first page, but do not use letterhead stationery.

- As in Figure 10.1, indicate the continuation page with the page number, the name of your correspondent, and the date. You may place this information in the header, as in Figure 10.1 or in the footer.

- Have at least three lines of text on the last continuation page before the complimentary close and whatever else follows.

- The last paragraph on the page that precedes the last continuation page should contain at least two lines.

Simplified Letters

The simplified letter (see Figure 10.3), as its name implies, is a simplified form of the standard letter. It always has a subject line, but it does not have either a salutation or a complimentary close. In every other respect, it follows the format of a standard letter.

Use a simplified letter for routine correspondence only when you do not have the name of a person to address. You could use it, for example, to register a complaint with an organization or to make a simple inquiry to some department within an organization. Do not use a simplified letter to answer complaints (where good strategy calls for you to address the person who is complaining by name) or for important letters like letter reports.

Memorandums

Memorandums are used for correspondence within an organization. They most often are written on printed forms that are headed with the organization's name and spaces for *date, to, from,* and *subject* (see Figure 10.4, p. 154). Because of the memo's format, a salutation and signature block are not needed. To sign a memo, employees at many organizations initial their names in the memo heading. The body of a memo and its continuation page look precisely like the body and continuation page of a letter. A memo also uses the same end notations as a letter.

Memos may be used for any of the purposes for which letters are used. That is, you can write memos that provide information or make inquiries or memo reports that, like letter reports, are short reports containing summaries, introductions, headings, and so forth.

Memo Format

Roswell Electric

Date: 12 February 2008

To: Tom Hovey
Vice President

From: Barbara Gamez *BG*
Plant Engineer

Subject: Improving Plant Power Consumption

An article in the January 2008 *Mechanical Engineering*
(pp. 62–63) describes how TU Electric was able to reduce
their plant's pumping power consumption significantly. Encor-
American Technologies, Inc., conducted field observations and
computer simulated flow studies that revealed turbulence in TU's
system was wasting power. Implementing changes recommended
by Encor reduced TU's power consumption by 9%.

   I recommend that we contact Encor and request a
consultation.

E-mail Format

To: thovey@Ru.org

Subject: Improving plant power consumption

Tom, an article in the January 2008 *Mechanical Engineering*
(pp. 62–63) describes how TU Electric was able to reduce their
plant's pumping power consumption significantly. Encor-
American Technologies, Inc., conducted field observations and
computer simulated flow studies that revealed turbulence in
TU's system was wasting power. Implementing changes
recommended by Encor reduced TU's power consumption by 9%.
I think we should contact Encor and request a consultation.
Barbara G.

FIGURE 10.4   Message in Memo and E-mail Formats

E-mail

The speed and simplicity of e-mail have led to its widespread use both inside and outside of organizations. In many instances, it has replaced telephone calls and short memos and letters. E-mail format is determined by the software application used, but most formats include blanks similar to memo entries for address, subject, message, and so forth (see Figure 10.4).

The messages sent by e-mail tend to be brief. When used among trusted colleagues, e-mail messages are likely to be highly informal and full of abbreviations and other shortcuts, perhaps known only to those sending and receiving them. However, when sending e-mail to authority figures or people you don't know well, be more circumspect.

If you do not save the e-mail messages you send and receive, you may face the same pitfall as with phone conversations: that is, people's memories of what was actually said or implied may differ widely. When using e-mail, it is important to remember how easily messages can be forwarded or sent accidently to others, especially if you do not carefully check names and e-mail addresses before you hit Send. Because everyone makes these common mistakes, work-related e-mails should never contain confidential or provocative messages. It is also generally considered unethical to send blind copies of e-mails. Individuals who receive blind copies are not identified on messages, so the directly addressed recipients are unaware that your message has been distributed to others. E-mail has become one of the most widely used methods for quickly communicating with others in the workplace, but you should compose your e-mail messages with the same attention to audience, purpose, and situation that you give to other writing tasks you complete.

Correspondence of the Job Search

Begin your job search correspondence by brainstorming the elements of your past education and job experience. With the help of college transcripts, memory, and any journals and records you had the foresight to keep, list details such as dates, job titles, course titles, professors' and employers' names, work accomplished, and so forth. Make your list as extensive as possible. The information you record will furnish material for résumés and letters of application, the two most important pieces of correspondence in a job search.

Résumés

A *résumé* is the summary of your education and job experience that you send to potential employers. Based on this and the accompanying letter of application, potential employers will decide whether to interview you. Thus, your résumé is a very important document. See Figures 10.5, 10.6, and 10.7 for example résumés (pp. 157–159).

The two most widely used kinds of résumés are *chronological* and *functional*. Both can be done in a standard paper format or in digital formats suitable for e-mailing or scanning.

Chronological Résumés Look at Figure 10.5. Begin a chronological résumé with your name and address and list all the ways you can be reached: mail, phone, fax, and e-mail. Next, give the details of your higher education: school or schools attended, degree, expected graduation date, major, minor, coursework, extracurricular activities, and so forth. Avoid the constant repetition of *I* by using fragmentary sentences.

You should indicate your academic standing in the most favorable way you legitimately can. If your GPA in your major is higher than your overall GPA, use that. If your record is really bad, don't list it. If you attended more than one college, list the last one first and so on.

Give the details of your work experience. As with your education, do it in reverse chronological order. Don't merely list job titles. Using action verbs like *managed, operated, organized, sold,* and *designed,* describe what you did. List all the jobs of your college years, even those that don't relate to the jobs you are seeking. Employers feel, quite correctly, that people who have worked understand the workplace better than those who have not.

If you have room, give a few details of your personal background. Sometimes, employers will see something there that interests them, particularly people skills, which they value highly.

Offer to supply references. Use both professors and employers (more on this later). Finish off with the month and year of the résumé.

The advantage of the chronological résumé is that it provides a smooth summary, year by year, of your education and experience. If there is growth, this type of résumé will show it well. But if your education and experience have big gaps, the chronological résumé may not be the best choice. Also, your skills and aptitudes may get lost in the welter of dates, courses, and jobs. Despite all that, the chronological résumé is a good format.

JANICE OSBORN
32 Merchant Road
St. Paul, MN 55101
Phone: (612) 555-6755
E-Mail: josborn@wave.com

Education **2004–2008**	**University of Minnesota, St. Paul, MN** Candidate for Bachelor of Science degree in Technical Communication with a minor in Computer Science in June 2008. In upper third of class with a GPA of 3.0 on a 4.0 scale. Member of St. Paul Student Council, vice president in senior year. Served as editorial assistant, 2006–2008 for *Technical Communication Quarterly*, the journal of the Association of Teachers of Technical Writing. Corresponded with authors and copyedited articles.
Business **Experience** **2007 Summer**	**Communication Design Associates,** **Minneapolis, MN** As part of five-person team, assisted large corporation in using SGML (Standard Generalized Markup Language) to convert 10,000 pages of paper documentation to online documentation.
2004–2005 **Summers**	**Technical Publications, Inc.** **Minneapolis, MN** Using desktop publishing techniques, worked collaboratively and individually in developing manuals, proposals, and feasibility reports.

FIGURE 10.5   Chronological Résumé

JANICE OSBORN
32 Merchant Road
St. Paul, MN 55101
Phone: (612) 555-6755
E-Mail: josborn@wave.com

Education	Candidate for Bachelor of Science degree in Technical Communication with a minor in Computer Science from University of Minnesota in June 2008.
Professional	• Working under pressure, used desktop publishing to produce high-quality manuals, proposals, and feasibility reports. • As part of five-person team, assisted large corporation in using SGML (Standard Generalized Markup Language) to convert 10,000 pages of paper documentation to online documentation. • Assisted editor of professional journal in copyediting manuscripts and corresponding with authors. • Completed courses in writing, editing, speaking, desktop publishing, graphics, management, multimedia, and computer science.
People	• Elected vice president of St. Paul Campus Student Council. Oversaw student recreational budget. • Successfully worked in collaboration with other writers and editors. • Accepted criticism and used it constructively.
Work Experience **2007 Summer**	• Communication Design Associates, Minneapolis, MN: Writer and member of consulting team.
2006–2008	• *Technical Communication Quarterly*, St. Paul Campus: Editorial Assistant.
2004–2005 Summers	• Technical Publications, Minneapolis, MN: Technical writer and editor.

FIGURE 10.6   **Functional Résumé**

JANICE OSBORN
32 Merchant Road
St. Paul, MN 55101
Phone: (612) 555-6755
E-Mail: josborn@wave.com

EDUCATION
University of Minnesota, St. Paul, MN, 2004–2008
Candidate for Bachelor of Science degree in Technical
Communication with a minor in Computer Science in June 2008.
In upper third of class with a GPA of 3.0 on a 4.0 scale.

Member of St. Paul Student Council, vice president in senior year.
Served as editorial assistant, 2006–2008 for Technical
Communication Quarterly, the Journal of the Association of
Teachers of Technical Writing. Corresponded with authors and
copyedited articles.

BUSINESS EXPERIENCE
Communication Design Associates
Minneapolis, MN, Summer 2007

As part of five-person team, assisted large corporation in using
SGML (Standard Generalized Markup Language) to convert 10,000
pages of paper documentation to online documentation.

Technical Publications, Inc.
St. Paul, MN, Summers 2004, 2005
Using desktop publishing techniques, worked collaboratively and
individually in developing manuals, proposals, and feasibility reports.

KEYWORDS
Technical communication, editing, SGML, documentation, desktop
publishing, manuals, proposals, reports

FIGURE 10.7   **Digital Résumé**

Functional Résumés Look at Figure 10.6. Begin a functional résumé with your name, address, phone number, and the like, as in the chronological résumé. Next, give your degree, major and minor, and expected graduation date. If you attended more than one college, give them in reverse chronological order.

The heart of a functional résumé is a classification of your experiences—academic, extracurricular, and work—that demonstrates your skills and capabilities. (See pp. 27–28 for the rules of classification.) Using category words such as *professional, technical, people, communication, management, marketing, sales,* and *research,* create two or three categories that show you off the best.

Finish the résumé with a reverse chronological listing of your jobs, an offer of references, and the date.

The advantage of the functional résumé is that it brings to the fore your skills and capabilities. There is a slight disadvantage in that it does not show the smooth progression of the chronological résumé. Choose the résumé that displays you to your best advantage.

Résumé Formats You have several options for delivering your résumé. If you are going to mail it through the postal service, you may use a standard format. However, if you know the employer is going to scan your résumé into a database, use a scannable digital format. If you are requested to send it via e-mail, also use a digital format.

Standard Format. In the standard format, you can take advantage of the font possibilities on a word processor, but use discretion and good page design (see Chapter 5). Don't fill your résumé with exotic typefaces. The mix of plain print and boldface in Figures 10.5 and 10.6 illustrates the look you want.

Résumés in any format must be mechanically perfect—no misspellings, typos, or grammatical errors. If you need help to accomplish this, get help.

When finished, print your résumé on good-quality white paper using a letter-quality printer. Never fold or staple your résumé. The best method for sending your résumé to a potential employer electronically is to save it in portable document format (PDF) and attach it to your e-mail message.

Digital Format. Figure 10.7 illustrates a digital résumé. Use a digital format to insert your résumé into an e-mail or when you know the potential employer will scan your résumé into a database. If you are uncertain as to whether an employer will want a scannable copy, send both standard and scannable résumés. You can attach the standard résumé as a PDF to your e-mail and paste your digital résumé into the e-mail message itself.

To ensure that your digital résumé can be read, you must use plain text. *Plain text,* absent any special formatting codes, can be read by any computer or scanner. Follow these guidelines in constructing your digital résumé:

- Do not use boldface, italics, underlining, or any of the other design features available on a word processor.
- Use single columns, aligned at the left, with no more than 65 characters per line.
- Use a standard width typeface—for example, Courier.
- Use capital letters when you want emphasis.
- Space with the space bar, not tabs.

When managers want to pull up résumés from a database, they will look for *keywords* that match terms used in the field in which the jobs are located. Look for keywords in job announcements for your field, and include them in your résumé.

If you e-mail your résumé, include your letter of application, constructed in a digital format, as part of your message. Indicate in the opening paragraph that you have attached a PDF of your résumé, so your attachment will not be considered a virus. If you mail your résumé through the postal service, print it and the accompanying letter of application on good-quality white paper. Do not fold or staple either one.

Letters of Application

When you send out your résumé, accompany it with a letter of application (see Figure 10.8, p. 162). The letter of application is a letter of transmittal for the résumé, but it is also a place where you can highlight your

32 Merchant Road
St. Paul, MN 55101
(612) 555-6755
josborn@wave.com
9 March 2008

Mr. James Cantrell
Supervisor of Writing and Publications
Bell Computer Corporation
4200 Lake Avenue
Madison, WI 53714

Dear Mr. Cantrell:

Professor Robert Wilson of the University of Minnesota Computer Science Department tells me that your firm designs communication protocols that allow two or more computer networks to operate as one network. This is a field of great interest to me, and I think I have the education and experience to serve Bell Computer well.

In June, I will graduate from the University's Technical Communication program with a minor in Computer Science. I have completed courses in writing, editing, speaking, desktop publishing, graphics, management, multimedia, and computer science.

In the summers of 2004 and 2005, I worked as a technical writer and editor using desktop publishing to produce high-quality manuals, proposals, and feasibility reports. Last summer, I worked on a team helping a large corporation use SGML to convert paper files into online files. This experience, combined with my education, would allow me to fit into your operation quickly.

The enclosed résumé gives more detailed information about my education and experience. I can provide references from both my instructors and employers.

May I come to Madison to discuss job opportunities with you? If that is not convenient, I'll be attending the International Technical Communication Conference in May. Perhaps we can talk there.

Sincerely yours,

Janice Osborn

Janice Osborn

Encl.

FIGURE 10.8   **Letter of Application**

capabilities and catch an employer's interest. If you are discreet about it, you can use your letter of application to point out how you could fit into the organization and why it would be to the employer's advantage to hire you. Blow your own horn, but not directly in the employer's ear.

If possible, send your letter and résumé to the person for whom you might work. A potential supervisor is better able to judge your qualifications than a human resources officer. Often, a letter or phone call to the organization might get you the name you need. Looking through professional journals in your field will often provide such names, as will networking with professionals. Web sites and forums on the Internet also provide useful information about employers. Send letters and résumés to human resources divisions if need be, but only as a last resort.

A good way to start your letter is by dropping a name known to the potential employer. However, do this only with permission. Indicate some knowledge of the organization, which you can gather in the same way as names. In the middle of the letter, *sell yourself.* Use specific education and work experiences to point out your potential value and usefulness to the organization.

In the close of the letter, refer to your résumé and references. If you have significant products from your work or education (such as research reports, manuals, videos, and so forth), offer to send them. Finally, try to arrange an interview. Make it as convenient for the employer as you possibly can.

Other Correspondence

Several other pieces of correspondence are necessary during the job search, none of them difficult or time-consuming to do.

When you ask your references for permission to use their names, provide them with copies of your résumé. If you can, call on them. If you can't, write each person a letter, recalling your relationship with him or her and asking for his or her permission.

Sending several thank-you notes is appropriate during and after the job search. When you interview, get the interviewer's name and address; later, write a note, expressing appreciation for the interview. When your job search succeeds, write thank-you notes to all your references. Share with them the outcome of the search, and thank them for their help. They will be curious about the result and pleased with your thoughtfulness.

If you are offered jobs at several organizations, drop a note of thanks and refusal to each of the organizations you turn down. Simply express your appreciation for the job offer, thank them for their time and interest, and perhaps compliment them on their organization.

Further Information

For additional information, go to http://www.bls.gov/OCO, a Bureau of Labor Web site. There you will find tools such as the *Occupational Outlook Handbook,* which describes in depth hundreds of occupations and provides useful information for the job search.

ACTIVITIES

1. Visit your institution's career center or placement office, and find out what resources are available for graduates. Bring to class job search materials that the center or office provides and discuss how they are similar and different from the guidelines described in this chapter.

2. Collect the letters you receive in the mail for three or four days, and bring them to class. What kinds of letters do you receive more frequently? What formats do they use? How do these letters compare with the e-mails you receive during the same time period?

CHAPTER ASSIGNMENTS

Assignment 1 for Individual Writers: The Résumé Set

Find a job ad for which you are currently qualified to apply. Write an application letter and résumé (either chronological or functional) to apply to the job. Create a print copy of both the application letter and résumé, and give these copies to your instructor. Then modify the print versions for e-mail delivery. Send the e-mail version to your instructor, and remember to attach your résumé in portable document format (PDF) or insert an electronic version into the body of the e-mail.

Chapter Notes

Chapter 3

[1]Adapted from Rebecca D. Williams, "FDA Proposes Folic Acid Fortification," *FDA Consumer* (May 1994): 13.

[2]Adapted from Dick Karsky, "Scarifiers for Shelterwoods," *Tree Planters' Notes* 44 (1993): 14.

Chapter 4

[1]Nyle K. Walton, "Demographic Issues," *Geographic and Global Issues* (Autumn 1993): 10–11.

[2]Mark Gerstein and Cyrus Chothia, "Proteins in Motion," *Science* (10 September 1999): 1683.

[3]Gil Lambany, Mario Renaud, and Michel Beauchesne, "Control of Growing Medium Water Content and Its Effect on Small Seedlings Grown in Large Containers," *Tree Planters' Notes* 48 (1997): 49.

[4]Kenneth E. Trenberth, "The Extreme Weather Events of 1997 and 1998," *Consequences: The Nature and Implications of Environmental Change* 5 (1999), http//:www.gorio.org/consequences/vol5no1/extreme.html (5 January 2000).

[5]Adapted from Trenberth.

Chapter 5

[1]Updates, *FDA Consumer* 4 (1999): 6.

Chapter 7

[1]For an extended look at the ethical principles discussed in this chapter, see R. John Brockmann and Fern Rook, eds., *Technical Communication and Ethics* (Washington, DC: Society for Technical Communication, 1989). In particular, see H. Lee Shimbergs' "Ethics and Rhetoric in Technical Writing," 59–62.

[2]The Online Ethics Center for Engineering and Ethics, http://onlineethics.org/ (12 January 2000).

[3]*The Chicago Manual of Style*, 15th ed. (Chicago: The University of Chicago Press, 2003), Chapter 16.

[4]For an excellent discussion of the principles discussed in this section, see Edward R. Tufte, *The Visual Display of Quantitative Information* (Cheshire, CT: Graphics Press, 1983), 53–87.

Chapter 8

[1]Adapted from Martin D. Tomasi and Brad Mehlenbacher, "Re-Engineering On-line Documentation," *Technical Communication* 46 (1999): 55.

[2]Ricki Lewis, "Surprise Cause of Gastritis Revolutionizes Ulcer Treatment," *FDA Consumer* 28 (1994): 18.

Chapter 9

[1]David L. Wenny, "Calculating Filled and Empty Cells Based on Number of Seeds per Cell: A Microcomputer Application," *Tree Planters' Notes* 44 (1993): 49.

[2]The fusion energy argument is based on FusEdWeb: Fusion Energy Education, http://fusedweb.llnl.gov. (2008).

Index